MY MUSLIM FRIENDS LEARN ABOUT JESUS

CHARLES MWEWA

MY MUSLIM FRIENDS LEARN ABOUT JESUS:

For Adjudicators and Claimants Who Seek Refugee Status on Account of Conversion to Christianity

Published by:

AFRICA IN CANADA PRESS

Ottawa, ON

Canada

www.acpress.ca

ISBN: 978-1-988251-89-9

DEDICATION

To all genuinely converted Christians who are being persecuted for their faith.

CONTENTS

AUTHOR'S WORD

For over six years, I have represented refugee claimants from Islamic nations who have been victims of brutal and targeted religious intolerance. When they explain their ordeals, one easily recognizes that, but for God's grace and mercy, they are alive. Some go through such hardships that it is hardly possible to find a correct term to describe them.

They are hated simply because they converted from one religion to Christianity. Canada, and similarly situated nations, fortunately, welcomes such religious refugees. Here, they find a home, a receptive safe haven and a place that has, truly, embraced the idea that, we can be different but still be respectful of our differences at the same time.

I have helped many people successfully defend their refugee claims at the Immigration and Refugee Board (IRB) of Canada, Refugee Protection Division (RPD) based on religion. This book is the publication of the materials I have used, and also the responses my clients have elicited at the RPD that have resulted in favorable outcomes. This is a practical tool; it has been tested and verified.

I have provided an entire *Gospel of John* in ***Appendix I***. This serves three purposes. First, the claimant has a ready text for reference. Second, most questions on the knowledge test in refugee claims are derived from the *Gospel of John*. And third, the *Gospel of John* is one of the best tools for new Christians to follow because of the narrative style in which it was written. The inclusion of the Gospel text in this book makes it a very user-friendly tool and a one-stop-shop for anyone wishing to make a success refugee claim based on religion anywhere in the world, especially in Canada.

cm.

1 | KNOWLEDGE TEST

Introduction

In this chapter, questions and answers based on the Bible are provided. While the author has made every effort to present in clear terms the appropriate responses based on his observations as he has represented refugee claimants in Canada, the answers are not exhaustive, and other interpretations may absolutely be possible. Claimants should consult their Church leaders when in doubt. However, everyone who responded as indicated in this book, succeeded in defending their claims on the knowledge test section.

Background to the Questions

God had promised a Messiah or Savior, who would save the world (people) from their sins and the impeding Hell fire.

About 700 years before Jesus Christ was born, Isaiah predicated His birth:

"Therefore the Lord himself will give you a sign: The virgin will conceive and give birth to a son, and will call him Immanuel."[1]

Matthew confirms that Immanuel means, "God is with us."

"The virgin will conceive and give birth to a son, and they will call him Immanuel (which means 'God with us')."[2]

The about 14-year old virgin who conceived and gave birth to a Messiah is Mary.

Joseph, a seventeen-year old boy, had betrothed Mary to be his wife (or had engaged Mary as his fiancée). But before the formal marriage ceremony was performed, that is, before they could sleep together, Joseph discovered that Mary was pregnant. Joseph, because he was a good and holy man, decided to end the engagement in secret. But before he could finally tell Mary that the engagement was off, he had a dream. In that dream, an angel, Gabriel, appeared to him and this is what the Bible records of that incident:

---

[1] Isaiah 7:14

[2] Matthew 1:23

> But after he had pondered these things, an angel of the Lord appeared to him in a dream and said, "Joseph, son of David, do not be afraid to embrace Mary as your wife, for the One conceived in her is from the Holy Spirit. She will give birth to a Son, and you are to give Him the name Jesus, *because He will save His people from their sins.*" All this took place to fulfill what the Lord had said through the prophet: "Behold, the virgin will be with child and will give birth to a son, and they will call Him Immanuel" (which means, "God with us").[3]

Key Question about Jesus Christ Answered:

Who is Jesus Christ?

Answer:

Jesus Christ is the promised Messiah, the Savior of mankind (people) from their sins and Hell fire. He is the Lord. He was born, so He is a Man. But because the power that caused His birth came from the Holy Spirit (God), He is also God. Jesus means "Savior."

---

[3] Matthew 1:20-23 (emphasis added)

Key Claims of Jesus Christ:

Jesus Christ claimed that He was from the beginning first as the Word and God: "In the beginning was the Word, and the Word was with God, and the Word was God."[4]

He claimed that He temporarily came to earth in the flesh, as a human being: "The Word became flesh and made his dwelling among us. We have seen his glory, the glory of the one and only Son, who came from the Father, full of grace and truth."[5]

He claimed, and others worshipped Him, as the Son of God: "Then those who were in the boat worshiped him, saying, 'Truly you are the Son of God.'"[6]

He claimed that He is the Way, the Truth and the Life, and that there is no other passage way to the Father (God) except through Him: "I am

---

[4] John 1:1
[5] John 1:14
[6] Matthew 14:33

Jesus Christ is the beginning and the end of the Christian faith, "Looking unto Jesus the author and finisher of our faith; who for the joy that was set before him endured the cross, despising the shame, and is set down at the right hand of the throne of God."[22]

Jesus Christ heals those who believe in Him, "But he was wounded for our transgressions, he was bruised for our iniquities: the chastisement of our peace was upon him; and with his stripes we are healed."[23]

Anyone who confesses (acknowledges and admits) Jesus Christ and believes in their hearts that God rose Him from the dead, they are saved and spared from Hell fire, "That if thou shalt confess with thy mouth the Lord Jesus, and shalt believe in thine heart that God hath raised him from the dead, thou shalt be saved."[24]

Christ is the demonstration of God's love, "And walk in love, as Christ also hath loved us,

---

[22] Hebrews 12:2
[23] Isaiah 53:5
[24] Romans 10:9

and hath given himself for us an offering and a sacrifice to God for a sweetsmelling savor."[25]

Jesus Christ and the Father are one, "Verily, verily, I say unto you, He that receiveth whomsoever I send receiveth me; and he that receiveth me receiveth him that sent me."[26]

Jesus Christ, like the Father, is the same always, "Jesus Christ the same yesterday, and today, and forever."[27]

Jesus Christ is God in the flesh, "And the Word was made flesh, and dwelt among us, (and we beheld his glory, the glory as of the only begotten of the Father,) full of grace and truth,"[28] and, "Let this mind be in you, which was also in Christ Jesus: Who, being in the form of God, thought it not robbery to be equal with God: But made himself of no reputation, and took upon him the form of a servant, and was made in the likeness of men: And being found in fashion as a man, he humbled himself, and

[25] Ephesians 5:2
[26] John 13:20
[27] Hebrews 13:8
[28] John 1:14

Jesus Christ is the beginning and the end of the Christian faith, "Looking unto Jesus the author and finisher of our faith; who for the joy that was set before him endured the cross, despising the shame, and is set down at the right hand of the throne of God."[22]

Jesus Christ heals those who believe in Him, "But he was wounded for our transgressions, he was bruised for our iniquities: the chastisement of our peace was upon him; and with his stripes we are healed."[23]

Anyone who confesses (acknowledges and admits) Jesus Christ and believes in their hearts that God rose Him from the dead, they are saved and spared from Hell fire, "That if thou shalt confess with thy mouth the Lord Jesus, and shalt believe in thine heart that God hath raised him from the dead, thou shalt be saved."[24]

Christ is the demonstration of God's love, "And walk in love, as Christ also hath loved us,

---

[22] Hebrews 12:2

[23] Isaiah 53:5

[24] Romans 10:9

and hath given himself for us an offering and a sacrifice to God for a sweetsmelling savor."[25]

Jesus Christ and the Father are one, "Verily, verily, I say unto you, He that receiveth whomsoever I send receiveth me; and he that receiveth me receiveth him that sent me."[26]

Jesus Christ, like the Father, is the same always, "Jesus Christ the same yesterday, and today, and forever."[27]

Jesus Christ is God in the flesh, "And the Word was made flesh, and dwelt among us, (and we beheld his glory, the glory as of the only begotten of the Father,) full of grace and truth,"[28] and, "Let this mind be in you, which was also in Christ Jesus: Who, being in the form of God, thought it not robbery to be equal with God: But made himself of no reputation, and took upon him the form of a servant, and was made in the likeness of men: And being found in fashion as a man, he humbled himself, and

[25] Ephesians 5:2
[26] John 13:20
[27] Hebrews 13:8
[28] John 1:14

them out of my Father's hand. I and my Father are one."[19]

God, the Creator, is the Father of Jesus Christ, "Blessed be God, even the Father of our Lord Jesus Christ, the Father of mercies, and the God of all comfort; Who comforteth us in all our tribulation, that we may be able to comfort them which are in any trouble, by the comfort wherewith we ourselves are comforted of God."[20]

Only through Jesus Christ is there salvation for the entire human race, "Be it known unto you all, and to all the people of Israel, that by the name of Jesus Christ of Nazareth, whom ye crucified, whom God raised from the dead, even by him doth this man stand here before you whole. This is the stone, which was set at naught of you builders, which is become the head of the corner. Neither is there salvation in any other: for there is none other name under heaven given among men, whereby we must be saved."[21]

---

[19] John 10:28-30
[20] 2 Corinthians 1:3-4
[21] Acts 4:10-12

Key Facts about Jesus Christ:

Jesus Christ died for humanity so that through Him they could be saved if they believe and confess Him. Jesus is the Son of God, "Whosoever shall confess that Jesus is the Son of God, God dwelleth in him, and he in God."[16]

As God's only begotten Son, Jesus Christ saves those who believe in Him, "For God so loved the world, that he gave his only begotten Son, that whosoever believeth in him should not perish, but have everlasting life."[17]

Through Jesus Christ, God's love is revealed, "In this was manifested the love of God toward us, because that God sent his only begotten Son into the world, that we might live through him."[18]

Jesus Christ gives eternal life, "And I give unto them eternal life; and they shall never perish, neither shall any man pluck them out of my hand. My Father, which gave them [to] me, is greater than all; and no man is able to pluck

---

[16] 1 John 4:15
[17] John 3:16
[18] 1 John 4:9

He claimed that He was the Door: "I am the door. If anyone enters by Me, he will be saved, and will go in and out and find pasture."[12]

He claimed that He was the Resurrection and the Life: "I am the resurrection and the life. He who believes in me will live, even though he dies; and whoever lives and believes in me will never die."[13]

He claimed that He could forgive sins: "Then Jesus said to her, 'Your sins are forgiven.'"[14] And Jesus also gave the authority to His disciples to forgive sins: "If you forgive anyone's sins, their sins are forgiven; if you do not forgive them, they are not forgiven."[15]

---

[12] John 10:9
[13] John 11:25-26
[14] Luke 7:48
[15] John 20:23

the way and the truth and the life. No one comes to the Father except through me."[7]

He claimed that He was the Bread of Life: "I am the bread of life. He who comes to me will never go hungry, and he who believes in me will never be thirsty.'"[8]

He claimed that He was the Light of the World: "When Jesus spoke again to the people, he said, 'I am the light of the world. Whoever follows me will never walk in darkness, but will have the light of life.'"[9]

He claimed that He was the Vine: "I am the vine; you are the branches. If a man remains in me and I in him, he will bear much fruit; apart from me you can do nothing."[10]

He claimed that He was the Good Shepherd: "I am the good shepherd. The good shepherd lays down his life for the sheep."[11]

---

[7] John 14:6
[8] John 6:35
[9] John 8:12
[10] John 15:5
[11] John 10:11

became obedient unto death, even the death of the cross."[29]

Jesus Christ is the conqueror of death, "O death, where is thy sting? O grave, where is thy victory? The sting of death is sin; and the strength of sin is the law. But thanks be to God, which giveth us the victory through our Lord Jesus Christ."[30]

Jesus Christ prayed for all believers, "Wherefore he is able also to save them to the uttermost that come unto God by him, seeing he ever liveth to make intercession for them."[31]

Jesus Christ made believers the light of the world, "Ye are the light of the world. A city that is set on a hill cannot be hid. Neither do men light a candle, and put it under a bushel, but on a candlestick; and it giveth light unto all that are in the house. Let your light so shine before men, that they may see your good works, and glorify your Father which is in heaven."[32]

---

[29] Philippians 2:5-8
[30] 1 Corinthians 15:55-57
[31] Hebrews 7:25
[32] Matthew 5:14-16

Jesus Christ has the name above all names, "Wherefore God also hath highly exalted him, and given him a name which is above every name: That at the name of Jesus every knee should bow, of things in heaven, and things in earth, and things under the earth; And that every tongue should confess that Jesus Christ is Lord, to the glory of God the Father."[33]

Jesus Christ is God's glory incarnate, "Jesus saith unto her, Said I not unto thee, that, if thou wouldest believe, thou shouldest see the glory of God?"[34]

Jesus Christ was the promised Savior, "For unto us a child is born, unto us a son is given and the government shall be upon his shoulder: and his name shall be called Wonderful, Counsellor, The Mighty God, The Everlasting Father, The Prince of Peace."[35]

Jesus Christ died and rose again for all the world, "For I delivered unto you first of all that which I also received, how that Christ died for our sins according to the scriptures; And that he

---

[33] Philippians 2:9-11
[34] John 11:40
[35] Isaiah 9:6

was buried, and that he rose again the third day according to the scriptures."[36]

Jesus Christ holds everlasting dominion, "I saw in the night visions, and, behold, one like the Son of man came with the clouds of heaven, and came to the Ancient of Days, and they brought him near before him. And there was given him dominion, and glory, and a kingdom, that all people, nations, and languages, should serve him: his dominion is an everlasting dominion, which shall not pass away, and his kingdom that which shall not be destroyed."[37]

Jesus Christ is the pioneer of the Christian faith, "Fixing our eyes on Jesus, the pioneer and perfecter of faith. For the joy set before him he endured the cross, scorning its shame, and sat down at the right hand of the throne of God."[38]

---

[36] 1 Corinthians 15:3-4
[37]Daniel 7:13-14
[38] Hebrews 12:2

Key Summaries:

1. Who is Jesus' heavenly father?

Answer: God, the Father

2. What is the name of Jesus' mother?

Answer: Mary, the Virgin

3. Was Mary a virgin when she had Jesus?

Answer: Yes.

4. How did a virgin have a baby?

Answer:

God, through the power of the Holy Spirit, came upon her.

5. What did Joseph want to do with Mary when he discovered that she was pregnant?

Answer:

He had a dream that Mary's Son would be the savior of the world.

6. In which town was Jesus Christ born?

Answer: Bethlehem.

7. Where did Joseph take Mary to live, and then when His life was threatened, to hide?

Answer: Nazareth; Egypt

8. Who is John the Baptist?

Answer:

Jesus Christ' cousin who was born six months before Jesus. He preached repentance and baptized people in River Jordan. When Jesus approached him, he said that he did not want Jesus to be baptized by him, saying that he was not even worth to untie Jesus' shoes. John lived in the desert (wilderness). He wore a camel-hair garment and a leather belt. And he ate only honey and wild locusts.

9. Who is John the Baptist's mother and father?

Answer: Mother: Elizabeth
Father: Zachariah

10. Who wanted Jesus Christ to die?

Answer:

The Jews – the Pharisees and teachers of the law.

11. Did Jesus perform miracles?

Answer: Yes.

12. Name some of the miracles?

Answer:

- Turning water into wine
- Walking on water
- Calming the wind (storm)
- Feeding 5000 people
- Giving sight to blind people
- Raising the dead to life

13. What is the name of the Roman Governor who permitted Jesus to be killed?

Answer: Pontius Pilate.

14. Who was King Herod?

Answer:

The *de facto* king imposed upon the Jews by the Romans. He wanted the three *Maji* (the wisemen from the East) to tell him about Jesus so he could kill Jesus.

15. Who was Herodias?

Answer:

She was King Herod's sister-in-law and Herod was having a sexual affair with her. She asked Herod for the head of John the Baptist after her daughter danced before Herod and was asked to name a gift.

16. What is a Sabbath?

Answer:

The seventh-day of the week, Saturday. It was a day of rest because on that day God had rested from creating the heavens and the earth.

17. What is water baptism?

Answer:

Being immersed in water as a sign of death and resurrection. Believers in Jesus Christ may undergo the waters of baptism as a formal process of being entered into Church membership. Spiritually, it is a Christian ritual which ushers believers into what is called the "Body of Christ." There are many methods of conducting the baptismal service. Some prefer a complete immersion in water as a symbol of dying and resurrecting to others who sprinkle water. Some Christian groups prefer to baptize babies to others who only baptize those who have an understanding of what baptism means. To the later, lessons may be taken just before baptism. In both cases, many Christian groups offer a certificate of baptism as a formal and legal piece of evidence of membership either in the local church or in the universal Body of Christ.

18. Did John baptize with water or with the Holy Spirit?

Answer: Water.

19. What did John say Jesus was going to baptize people with?

Answer: The Holy Spirit and fire.

20. Was Jesus Christ baptized in water?

Answer: Yes.

21. Who baptized Jesus Christ in water?

Answer: John the Baptist

22. In which river did John baptize Jesus?

Answer: In the River Jordan.

23. What happened at Jesus' baptismal ceremony?

Answer:

John saw Jesus coming. John did not want to baptize Jesus because John knew that Jesus was God and that John did not count himself worthy to baptize his creator. But Jesus told John to continue baptizing Him in order to fulfil all righteousness. At that time, while in the flesh and before His death and resurrection, Jesus was still under the Law of Moses and all its ceremonies. This, further, proved that Jesus was also a Man, not just God. Then God the Holy Spirit, in the form of a dove, came upon Jesus and John heard a voice from Heaven saying, "This is my beloved Son in whom I am well pleased."

24. Around what age was Jesus when he was crucified?

Answer: He was 33 years old.

25. Who betrayed Jesus?

Answer: Jesus was betrayed by Judas Iscariot.

26. For how many pieces of silver was Jesus betrayed (sold)?

Answer:

For 30 pieces of silver. Judas was, later, overcome with guilt for betraying Jesus. He threw the 30 silver coins into the temple. The Jewish leaders used the 30 pieces of silver to buy a field from a potter. Judas hanged himself (committed suicide) in that same field.

27. How many disciples did Jesus have?

Answer: 12.

28. What were the names of Jesus' disciples?

Answer:

Andrew
Bartholomew (Nathaniel)
James Alpheus
James Zebedee
John Zebedee
Judas Alpheus
Judas Iscariot
Matthew Levi
Philip
Simon Peter
Thaddaeus (Jude)
Thomas Didymus

29. Which disciple rejected Jesus three times, and which one doubted Him?

Answer: Simon Peter (rejected Jesus)
Thomas (doubted Jesus)

30. Name the garden Jesus prayed in three times before he went to the cross.

Answer: Gethsemane

31. How many days was Jesus dead?

Answer: 3 days

32. Who was Lazarus?

Answer:

Jesus' cousin who had been dead for four days.

33. Who were Lazarus' two sisters?

Answer: Martha and Mary

34. What did Jesus say at Lazarus' grave?

Answer:

Jesus went to his tomb and said "Lazarus, come forth"?

35. What is the meaning of Salvation.

Answer:

Salvation means that a person has believed in Jesus Christ as their personal Lord and Savior by repenting of their sins, believing and confessing that Jesus Christ is Lord, and accepting the free gift of Eternal Life, which is Christ. This is usually done by confessing or professing with the mouth and by a strong internal witness of the personal spirit that one has rejected the evil world and accepted the promise of an everlasting life after death. This process may also be termed, "Conversion."

36. What is Sin?

Answer:

Sin is both a state and a condition. All humans are presumed to be in a state of sin; they are born in sin according to the Bible:

"Behold, I was brought forth in iniquity,
And in sin my mother conceived me."[39]

But sin is also a condition; people may deliberately choose to sin (disobedience):

"The one who sins is the one who will die. The child will not share the guilt of the parent, nor will the parent share the guilt of the child. The righteousness of the righteous will be credited to them, and the wickedness of the wicked will be charged against them."[40]

Sin is defined in the Bible, as the transgression (violation or breaking) of the law:

---

[39] Psalm 51:5

[40] Ezekiel 18:20

"Whosoever committeth sin transgresseth also the law: *for sin is the transgression of the law.*"[41]

In short, Sin is when someone knows the good they must do but, rather, choose to do the bad or evil. The Bible mentions many varieties of sins (or works of the flesh), including: "…sexual immorality, impurity, sensuality, idolatry, sorcery, enmity, strife, jealousy, fits of anger, rivalries, dissensions, divisions, envy, drunkenness, orgies, and things like these."[42]

However, there has been a modification to the definition of Sin under the law and the one under grace. Since the resurrection of Jesus Christ ushered in a new dispensation of grace (basically absence of law), Sin is no longer the breaking of the law, because there is no law to break. Under grace, everything is permitted: "'I have the right to do anything,' you say—but not everything is beneficial. 'I have the right to do anything'—but I will not be mastered by anything."[43] What is Sin, therefore, is anything that is not beneficial to you and to your neighbor. If what you do or say or your

---

[41] 1 John 3:4 (emphasis added)
[42] Galatians 5:19-21
[43] 1 Corinthians 6:12

attitude is not beneficial to you or your neighbor, then doing it is Sin to you. Therefore, "If anyone, then, knows the good they ought to do and doesn't do it, it is sin for them."[44]

This means that, unlike in the Old Testament and in our legal systems where there was and there is a national, public deterrent system that classifies certain behaviors as wrongs (sins), under grace, such facility does not exist anymore. Sin is individualized. It is a matter of our hearts, of our consciences: "If our hearts condemn us, we know that God is greater than our hearts, and he knows everything."[45] In other words, if your heart condemns you, you have sinned, if it doesn't, you haven't sinned. Similarly, if what you contemplate to do or say or your attitude will make another person stumble, then don't do or say or behave it.[46] Ultimately, the only sin that takes people to Hell is because they do not or did not believe in Jesus.[47]

---

[44] James 4:17
[45] 1 John 3:20
[46] See also Romans 14:19-21
[47] See John 16:9

37. What is Forgiveness?

Answer:

Forgiveness is letting go of the wrongs others have done against you. In Christianity, it is mandatory and compulsory for every Christian to forgive others. It is also a condition of one's own forgiveness from God: "[Forgive and you shall be forgiven] For if you forgive other people when they sin against you, your heavenly Father will also forgive you."[48]

38. What is Redemption?

Answer:

Redemption is a system that was followed in slavery times. It was an act of buying back the property that one had lost or sold. To do so, a ramson was required. Thus, a former slave owner would redeem his former slave if they so wanted them very much.

In the Bible, with modification, this process was engaged in to save humanity from the clutches of sin and the devil. It is premised

48 Matthew 6:14

upon the ground that humanity sold its birthright for dominion and rule over God's creation to Satan. This happened in the Garden of Eden – when the first couple, Adam and Eve, succumbed to Satan (serpent)'s temptation to eat from the Tree of Knowledge of Good and Evil. When they did, they willingly sold their power and authority to Satan. God could not give that power and authority back to mankind because humanity gave it willingly to Satan. God needed a human agent to do so. But no human being was worthy because they all had sinned.[49] Hence, God took the form of Man and paid with His own blood to redeem mankind. This process of Jesus Christ becoming flesh, living a sinless life, shedding His own blood and dying on the Cross, is called *Redemption*. In the end, it was the Man (Jesus Christ) who claimed back His power and authority by paying with His own life. Jesus Christ did not just die; He also rose again from the dead. By rising, Jesus Christ gave a strong witness to the redemption process and secured for humanity a permanent right over the dominion of the earth, as it was originally intended. Thus, everyone who believes in Jesus Christ will rise again from the

[49] See Romans 3:23

dead in order to continue their rightful domination of the earth: "Here is a trustworthy saying: If we died with him, we will also live with him."[50]

39. What is Holy Communion?

Answer:

It is also called *The Last Supper* or the *Eucharist.* It was the last meal Jesus Christ had with His disciples. In it, Jesus Christ announced (proclaimed) a New Covenant which would be based upon His blood. Through it, He also ushered in the Church, the Body of Christ. Bread was broken, symbolizing Jesus' broken body, and wine was drunk, symbolizing Jesus' spilled blood. The Bible summarizes it, thus:

> For I received from the Lord Himself that [instruction] which I passed on to you, that the Lord Jesus on the night in which He was betrayed took bread; and when He had given thanks, He broke it and said, "This is (represents) My body, which is [offered as a sacrifice] for you. Do this in [affectionate] remembrance of Me." In the same way, after supper

[50] 2 Timothy 2:11

> He took the cup, saying, "This cup is the new covenant [ratified and established] in My blood; do this, as often as you drink it, in [affectionate] remembrance of Me." For every time you eat this bread and drink this cup, you are [symbolically] proclaiming [the fact of] the Lord's death until He comes [again].
>
> So, then whoever eats the bread or drinks the cup of the Lord in a way that is unworthy [of Him] will be guilty of [profaning and sinning against] the body and blood of the Lord. But a person must [prayerfully] examine himself [and his relationship to Christ], and only when he has done so should he eat of the bread and drink of the cup. For anyone who eats and drinks [without solemn reverence and heartfelt gratitude for the sacrifice of Christ], eats and drinks a judgment on himself if he does not [b]recognize the body [of Christ].[51]

And Jesus Christ Himself gave a command that this (Communion) should be done frequently in remembrance of Him till His return: "…and when he had given thanks, he broke it and said, 'This is my body, which is

[51] 1 Corinthians 11:23-29 (Amplified Bible)

for you; do this in remembrance of me....This cup is the new covenant in My blood; do this, as often as you drink it, in remembrance of Me.'"[52] Some Christian groups (also called denominations) do this every Sunday when they meet for mass; others do so occasionally during their Church services.

40. What is Resurrection?

Answer:

This is one of the central tenets of the Christian faith and doctrine. It is the doctrine (creed) of rising back to life after death. Christians believe that Jesus Christ died and came back to life again by the power of the Holy Spirit. They also believe that since Jesus rose again from the dead, they will also be raised from the dead at the end of the age. Apostle Paul argues that, if the resurrection doesn't exist, Christianity doesn't exist, either: "And if Christ has not been raised, our preaching is useless and so is your faith."[53] The implication is that, there is a resurrection.

---

[52] 1 Corinthians 11:24-25

[53] 1 Corinthians 15:14

41. What is Rapture?

Answer:

Christian believers believe that when Jesus comes again for the second time, He will first "rapture," or take out of the earth in bodily form, all those who had died in faith and those who will be alive. This elation of believers in the air is called a Rapture. Apostle Paul declares it this way:

> For the Lord Himself will descend from heaven with a loud command, with the voice of an archangel, and with the trumpet of God, and the dead in Christ will be the first to rise. After that, we who are alive and remain will be caught up together with them in the clouds to meet the Lord in the air. And so we will always be with the Lord.[54]

[54] 1 Thessalonians 4:16-17

42. What is Revelation?

Answer:

In his old age, Apostle John, the beloved, was arrested and imprisoned on a Greek island called Patmos. John writes, "I, John, both your brother and companion in tribulation, was on the island that is called Patmos for the word of God and for the testimony of Jesus Christ."[55] It was during that time that John wrote the last book of the New Testament Bible called "Revelation." It is the further revelation of Jesus Christ and of the end days and of what will follow.

43. What is Repentance?

Answer:

Repentance means to turn away from sin. Biblically, this means to stop living an evil life and to begin living a righteous life. It is believed to be the first step into conversion.

---

[55] Revelation 1:9

44. What is a Trinity?

Answer:

Christians believe that God is a triune God – the Father, the Son (Jesus Christ) and the Holy Spirit. "But for us, there is one God, the Father, by whom all things were created, and for whom we live. And there is one Lord, Jesus Christ, through whom all things were created, and through whom we live."[56] God is also the Spirit: "Now the Lord is the Spirit, and where the Spirit of the Lord is, there is freedom."[57] And these three are One: "May the grace of the Lord Jesus Christ, and the love of God, and the fellowship of the Holy Spirit be with you all."[58]

45. Who killed Jesus?

Answer:

The Romans did the actual killing. However, it was the Jews who demanded for His death.

---

[56] 1 Corinthians 8:6
[57] 2 Corinthians 3:17
[58] 2 Corinthians 13:14

46. Did the Jews accept Jesus as their Savior?

Answer:

There was mixed views among the Jews concerning the deity of Jesus Christ. Some, like among His own disciples, willingly accepted Him as the promised Messiah. However, some of the nobilities and the teachers of the law and the Pharisees, rejected Him as Messiah.

47. Who is Barabbas?

Answer:

The criminal the Jews asked to be released instead of Jesus.

48. What are the Beatitudes?

Answer:

The sermon on the mountain and the happy (blessed) attitudes. They are contained in these refrains:[59]

---

[59] Matthew 5:3-12

Blessed are the poor in spirit,
  for theirs is the kingdom of heaven.
Blessed are those who mourn,
  for they will be comforted.
Blessed are the meek,
  for they will inherit the earth.
Blessed are those who hunger and thirst for righteousness,
  for they will be filled.
Blessed are the merciful,
  for they will be shown mercy.
Blessed are the pure in heart,
  for they will see God.
Blessed are the peacemakers,
  for they will be called children of God.
Blessed are those who are persecuted because of righteousness,
  for theirs is the kingdom of heaven.
Blessed are you when people insult you, persecute you and falsely say all kinds of evil against you because of me. Rejoice and be glad, because great is your reward in heaven, for in the same way they persecuted the prophets who were before you.

49. What is Heaven?

Answer:

The place of God's abode, and where the souls of the saints are expected to go. During the Old Testament, God revealed that Heaven was His throne: "This is what the LORD says: "Heaven is my throne, and the earth is my footstool. Where is the house you will build for me? Where will my resting place be?"[60] Jesus claimed that He came down from there: "For I have *come down from heaven*, not to do My own will, but the will of Him who sent Me."[61] The phrase, "come down from heaven,' has a connotation that Heaven is above, and the earth is below, and Hell is under the earth.

50. What is Hell?

Answer:

The place of torment and fire without end. Jesus Christ said that Hell was a place of torture: "Don't fear those who kill the body,

[60] Isaiah 66:1

[61] John 6:38 (emphasis added).

rather fear Him who is able to destroy both soul and body in hell."[62]

51. How does one become a Christian?

Answer:

By grace (God's unmerited favor) through faith in Jesus Christ.[63] One must believe in their hearts and confess with their mouths that Jesus Christ is Lord. For "Everyone who calls on the name of the Lord will be saved."[64]

However, there is no formulae as to how different people become Christians. God is Sovereign, and in His sovereignty, He may accept people in different ways. The central belief for all who have ever believed in Jesus Christ and converted into Christianity is that they saw a need for their sins to be forgiven and they called upon Jesus Christ to save them. In short, they *believe* in Jesus Christ.

---

[62] Matthew 10:28; Matthew 5:29-30; 23:15,33; and Luke 10:15; 16:23

[63] Ephesians 2:8-9

[64] Romans 10:13

52. What are the fruits of being a converted Christian?

Answer:

The Bible has given a guidance on this, and it is included in what is known as the *Fruit of the Spirit*: "But the fruit of the Spirit is love, joy, peace, forbearance, kindness, goodness, faithfulness, gentleness, and self-control. Against such things there is no law."[65] The rendition "fruit" (singular) is supported by the New Living Translation of Matthew 7:16: "You can identify them by their *fruit*, that is, by the way they act. Can you pick grapes from thornbushes, or figs from thistles?" (Emphasis added).

This may mean that a Christian produces one kind of a fruit with different parts. It may also mean that a Christian produces different kinds of fruits with different tastes. What is clear, however, is the fact that whatever a genuinely converted Christian produces is true, noble, right, pure, lovely, admirable, excellent or praiseworthy.[66]

---

[65] Galatians 5:22-23

[66] Philippians 4:8

A person who claims to have been genuinely converted to Christianity but who fails to produce the *fruit* or *fruits* as tabulated above, may put their Christianity in question, and, therefore, in doubt.

2| CREDEBILITY TEST

Introduction to Credibility

It is important to note that the credibility (truthfulness) of a testimony is more important than the knowledge test. It is possible that someone is lying but still answering all the knowledge test questions correctly. The decision-maker (adjudicator or "Member") is the trier of credibility. Only the decision-maker can discern whether a claimant is lying or telling the truth. It is also possible that some might fail the knowledge test and still be found credible. But it is also, sadly, possible, that someone is telling the truth, and still fails the knowledge test or is found not to be credible.

The real test, therefore, is to know and to effectively tell the truth. This little book will show you how to both ace the knowledge questions and effectively be credible. You are credible because you are telling the truth. While the knowledge test is abstract, the credibility test is practical.

Credibility: Practical Matters

Those who claim to have been converted will also demonstrate the following:

1. That they have actioned their faith. This means that they have one or more of the following:

    - They have found a home Church where they go to for worship, service or mass;

    - They have registered or a taking early beginners courses at their local Church;

    - They may be receiving instructions on baptism;

    - They are known by, at least, the leader or leaders of the Church branch where they attend for devotion and homage;

- They know the actual physical place (address) where they meet for services; address, contact details and other coordinates related to direction. If they attend remotely, they should provide evidence that they, actually, participate in those meetings. Evidence may be either photographic or witness testimony or both.

2. They should show evidence of conversion in their day-to-day Christian walk. This includes but is not limited to the following:

    - They pray often

    - They read the Bible frequently

    - They participate in community programs that their local Church undertakes

- They have been registered in at least one ministries or departments of the local Church

- They can point on at least one practical way in which their new faith is meaningful to them. This may include but is not limited to:

    - They don't curse any more

    - They are more loving to their family members

    - They spontaneously assist strangers who may need help

    - They may be volunteering in senior homes or hospices

- They are not given to hate or discrimination any longer

- They have forgiven even their worst enemies

- They may have an online spiritual activism they undertake if it does not put them in danger

- They may have a time-table for Bible study

- They may be involved in missionary activities

- They may be giving tithes and offerings to their local Church

- They are making practical efforts to stop the bad habits they used to do before conversion

- They confess their sins and ask for forgiveness both from God and from those around them whom they, inadvertently, offend

- They do not deliberately lie. It is important to note that even strong believers in Christ may lie from time to time. However, the difference with all others is that true converted believers do not lie on purpose.

3. They should delineate the efficacy of the new religion from the old one or old lifestyle. This can be demonstrated through making

contrasts. And this may include the following:

- In their old religion or faith, they did things as a routine; now they do things as matter of commitment and heart

- In their old religion or faith, they were not free; now they have experience real freedom, such as men and women participating in activities together, a sense of being needed and wanted, being given leading roles, and etc.

- In their old religion or faith, they were abused (verbally, physically, mentally or even sexually); now they are respected and such abuses are proscribed.

- In their old religion or faith, they were taught to resort to violence with violence; in Christianity, they forgive, and even love, their enemies. They may also turn another cheek to those who castigate them. It is important to note here that this does not mean to want to be abused or persecuted. Such refugee claimants have escaped their old religion on account of persecution, in the first place.

4. LOVE: Is the ultimate sign that one's conversion to Christianity is genuine. A claimant should be ready to give proof that since converting, their life revolves around love.

APPENDIX I

THE GOSPEL ACCORDING TO ST. JOHN

Chapter 1

[1:1] In the beginning was the Word, and the Word was with God, and the Word was God. [1:2] The same was in the beginning with God. [1:3] All things were made by him; and without him was not anything made that was made. [1:4] In him was life; and the life was the light of men. [1:5] And the light shineth in darkness; and the darkness comprehended it not.

[1:6] There was a man sent from God, whose name [was] John. [1:7] The same came for a witness, to bear witness of the Light, that all [men] through him might believe. [1:8] He was not that Light, but [was sent] to bear witness of that Light. [1:9] [That] was the true Light, which lighteth every man that cometh into the world. [1:10] He was in the world, and the world was made by him, and the world knew him not. [1:11] He came unto his own, and his own received him not. [1:12] But as many as received him, to them gave he power to become the sons of God, [even] to them that believe on his name: [1:13] Which were born, not of blood, nor of the will of the flesh, nor of the will of man, but of God. [1:14] And the Word was made flesh, and dwelt among us, (and we beheld his glory, the glory as of the only begotten of the Father,) full of grace and truth.

[1:15] John bare witness of him, and cried, saying, This was he of whom I spake, He that cometh after me is preferred before me: for he was before me. [1:16] And of his fulness have all we received, and grace for grace. [1:17] For the law was given by Moses, [but] grace and truth came by Jesus Christ. [1:18] No man hath seen God at any time; the only begotten Son, which is in the bosom of the Father, he hath declared [him][1:19] And this is the record of John, when the Jews sent priests and Levites from Jerusalem to ask him, Who art thou? [1:20] And he confessed, and denied not; but confessed, I am not the Christ. [1:21] And they asked him, What then? Art thou Elias? And he saith, I am not. Art thou that prophet? And he answered, No. [1:22] Then said they unto him, Who art thou? that we may give an answer to them that sent us. What sayest thou of thyself? [1:23] He said, I [am] the voice of one crying in the wilderness, Make straight the way of the Lord, as said the prophet Esaias.[1:24] And they which were sent were of the Pharisees.[1:25] And they asked him, and said unto him, Why baptizest thou then, if thou be not that Christ, nor Elias, neither that prophet? [1:26] John answered them, saying, I baptize with water: but there standeth one among you, whom ye know not; [1:27] He it is, who coming after me is preferred before me, whose shoe's latchet I am not worthy to unloose. [1:28] These things were done in Bethabara beyond Jordan, where John was baptizing.

[1:29] The next day John seeth Jesus coming unto him, and saith, Behold the Lamb of God, which taketh away the sin of the world. [1:30] This is he of whom I said, After me cometh a man which is preferred before me: for he was before me. [1:31] And I knew him not: but that he should be made manifest to Israel, therefore am I come baptizing with water. [1:32] And John bare record, saying, I saw the Spirit descending from heaven like a dove, and it abode upon him. [1:33] And I knew him not: but he that sent me to baptize with water, the same said unto me, Upon whom thou shalt see the Spirit descending, and remaining on him, the same is he which baptizeth with the Holy Ghost. [1:34] And I saw, and bare record that this is the Son of God.

[1:35] Again the next day after John stood, and two of his disciples; [1:36] And looking upon Jesus as he walked, he saith, Behold the Lamb of God! [1:37] And the two disciples heard him speak, and they followed Jesus. [1:38] Then Jesus turned, and saw them following, and saith unto them, What seek ye? They said unto him, Rabbi, (which is to say, being interpreted, Master,) where dwellest thou?[1:39] He saith unto them, Come and see. They came and saw where he dwelt, and abode with him that day: for it was about the tenth hour. [1:40] One of the two which heard John [speak,] and followed him, was Andrew, Simon Peter's brother. [1:41] He first findeth his own brother Simon, and saith unto him, We have found the Messias, which is, being interpreted, the Christ. [1:42] And he brought him to Jesus. And when Jesus beheld him, he said, Thou art Simon the son of Jona: thou shalt be called Cephas, which is by i[1:43] The day following Jesus would go forth into Galilee, and findeth Philip, and saith unto him, Follow me.[1:44] Now Philip was of Bethsaida, the city of Andrew and Peter. [1:45] Philip findeth Nathanael, and saith unto him, We have found him, of whom Moses in the law, and the prophets, did write, Jesus of Nazareth, the son of Joseph.[1:46] And Nathanael said unto him, Can there any good thing come out of Nazareth? Philip saith unto him, Come and see. [1:47] Jesus saw Nathanael coming to him, and saith of him, Behold an Israelite indeed, in whom is no guile! [1:48] Nathanael saith unto him, Whence knowest thou me? Jesus answered and said unto him, Before that Philip called thee, when thou wast under the fig tree, I saw thee. [1:49] Nathanael answered and saith unto him, Rabbi, thou art the Son of God; thou art the King of Israel. [1:50] Jesus answered and said unto him, Because I said unto thee, I saw thee under the fig tree, believest thou? thou shalt see greater things than these. [1:51] And he saith unto him, Verily, verily, I say unto you, Hereafter ye shall see heaven open, and the angels of God ascending and descending upon the Son of man.

Chapter 2

[2:1] And the third day there was a marriage in Cana of Galilee; and the mother of Jesus was there: [2:2] And both Jesus was called, and his disciples, to the marriage. [2:3] And when they wanted wine, the mother of Jesus saith unto him, They have no wine. [2:4] Jesus saith unto her, Woman, what have I to do with thee? mine hour is not yet come. [2:5] His mother saith unto the servants, Whatsoever he saith unto you, do [it.][2:6] And there were set there six waterpots of stone, after the manner of the purifying of the Jews, containing two or three firkins apiece. [2:7] Jesus saith unto them, Fill the waterpots with water. And they filled them up to the brim. [2:8] And he saith unto them, Draw out now, and bear unto the governor of the feast. And they bare [it.][2:9] When the ruler of the feast had tasted the water that was made wine, and knew not whence it was:(but the servants which drew the water knew;) the governor of the feast called the bridegroom, [2:10] And saith unto him, Every man at the beginning doth set forth good wine; and when men have well drunk, then that which is worse:[but] thou hast kept the good wine until now. [2:11] This beginning of miracles did Jesus in Cana of Galilee, and manifested forth his glory; and his disciples believed on him.

[2:12] After this he went down to Capernaum, he, and his mother, and his brethren, and his disciples: and they continued there not many days.

[2:13] And the Jews' passover was at hand, and Jesus went up to Jerusalem, [2:14] And found in the temple those that sold oxen and sheep and doves, and the changers of money sitting: [2:15] And when he had made a scourge of small cords, he drove them all out of the temple, and the sheep, and the oxen; and poured out the changers' money, and overthrew the tables; [2:16] And said unto them that sold doves, Take these things hence; make not my Father's house an house of merchandise. [2:17] And his disciples remembered that it was written, The zeal of thine house hath eaten me up.

[2:18] Then answered the Jews and said unto him, What sign shewest thou unto us, seeing that thou doest these things? [2:19] Jesus answered and said unto them, Destroy this temple, and in three days I will raise it up. [2:20] Then said the Jews, Forty and six years was this temple in building, and wilt thou rear it up in three days? [2:21] But he spake of the temple of his body. [2:22] When therefore he was risen from the dead, his disciples remembered that he had said this unto them; and they believed the scripture, and the word which Jesus had said.

[2:23] Now when he was in Jerusalem at the passover, in the feast [day,] many believed in his name, when they saw the miracles which he did. [2:24] But Jesus did not commit himself unto them, because he knew all [men,][2:25] And needed not that any should testify of man: for he knew what was in man.

Chapter 3

[3:1] There was a man of the Pharisees, named Nicodemus, a ruler of the Jews: [3:2] The same came to Jesus by night, and said unto him, Rabbi, we know that thou art a teacher come from God: for no man can do these miracles that thou doest, except God be with him. [3:3] Jesus answered and said unto him, Verily, verily, I say unto thee, Except a man be born again, he cannot see the kingdom of God. [3:4] Nicodemus saith unto him, How can a man be born when he is old? can he enter the second time into his mother's womb, and be born? [3:5] Jesus answered, Verily, verily, I say unto thee, Except a man be born of water and [of] the Spirit, he cannot enter into the kingdom of God. [3:6] That which is born of the flesh is flesh; and that which is born of the Spirit is spirit. [3:7] Marvel not that I said unto thee, Ye must be born again.[3:8] The wind bloweth where it listeth, and thou hearest the sound thereof, but canst not tell whence it cometh, and whither it goeth: so is every one that is born of the Spirit.[3:9] Nicodemus answered and said unto him, How can these things be? [3:10] Jesus answered and said unto him, Art thou a master of Israel, and knowest not these things?[3:11] Verily, verily, I say unto thee, We speak that we do know, and testify that we have seen; and ye receive not our witness. [3:12] If I have told you earthly things, and ye believe not, how shall ye believe, if I tell you [of] heavenly things? [3:13] And no man hath ascended up to heaven, but he that came down from heaven, [even] the Son of man which is in heaven.

[3:14] And as Moses lifted up the serpent in the wilderness, even so must the Son of man be lifted up:[3:15] That whosoever believeth in him should not perish, but have eternal life.

[3:18] He that believeth on him is not condemned: but he that believeth not is condemned already, because he hath not believed in the name of the only begotten Son of God.[3:19] And this is the condemnation, that light is come into the world, and men loved darkness rather than light, because their deeds were evil. [3:20] For every one that doeth evil hateth the light, neither cometh to the light, lest his deeds should be reproved. [3:21] But he that doeth truth cometh to the light, that his deeds may be made manifest, that they are wrought in God.

[3:22] After these things came Jesus and his disciples into the land of Judaea; and there he tarried with them, and baptized.

[3:23] And John also was baptizing in Aenon near to Salim, because there was much water there: and they came, and were baptized. [3:24] For John was not yet cast into prison.

[3:25] Then there arose a question between [some] of John's disciples and the Jews about purifying. [3:26] And they came unto John, and said unto him, Rabbi, he that was with thee beyond Jordan, to whom thou barest witness, behold, the same baptizeth, and all [men] come to him.[3:27] John answered and said, A man can receive nothing, except it be given him from heaven. [3:28] Ye yourselves bear me witness, that I said, I am not the Christ, but that I am sent before him. [3:29] He that hath the bride is the bridegroom: but the friend of the bridegroom, which standeth and heareth him, rejoiceth greatly because of the bridegroom's voice: this my joy therefore is fulfilled.[3:30] He must increase, but I [must] decrease. [3:31] He that cometh from above is above all: he that is of the earth is earthly, and speaketh of the earth: he that cometh from heaven is above all. [3:32] And what he hath seen and heard, that he testifieth; and no man receiveth his testimony.[3:33] He that hath received his testimony hath set to his seal that God is true. [3:34] For he whom God hath sent speaketh the words of God: for God giveth not the Spirit by measure [unto him.][3:35] The Father loveth the Son, and hath given all things into his hand. [3:36] He that believeth on the Son hath everlasting life: and he that believeth not the Son shall not see life; but the wrath of God abideth on him.

Chapter 4

[4:1] When therefore the Lord knew how the Pharisees had heard that Jesus made and baptized more disciples than John, [4:2] (Though Jesus himself baptized not, but his disciples,) [4:3] He left Judaea, and departed again into Galilee. [4:4] And he must needs go through Samaria.[4:5] Then cometh he to a city of Samaria, which is called Sychar, near to the parcel of ground that Jacob gave to his son Joseph. [4:6] Now Jacob's well was there. Jesus therefore, being wearied with [his] journey, sat thus on the well: [and] it was about the sixth hour. [4:7] There cometh a woman of Samaria to draw water: Jesus saith unto her, Give me to drink. [4:8] (For his disciples were gone away unto the city to buy meat.) [4:9] Then saith the woman of Samaria unto him, How is it that thou, being a Jew, askest drink of me, which am a woman of Samaria? for the Jews have no dealings with the Samaritans. [4:10] Jesus answered and said unto her, If thou knewest the gift of God, and who it is that saith to thee, Give me to drink; thou wouldest have asked of him, and he would have given thee living water.

[4:11] The woman saith unto him, Sir, thou hast nothing to draw with, and the well is deep: from whence then hast thou that living water? [4:12] Art thou greater than our father Jacob, which gave us the well, and drank thereof himself, and his children, and his cattle?[4:13] Jesus answered and said unto her, Whosoever drinketh of this water shall thirst again: [4:14] But whosoever drinketh of the water that I shall give him shall never thirst; but the water that I shall give him shall be in him a well of water springing up into everlasting life.[4:15] The woman saith unto him, Sir, give me this water, that I thirst not, neither come hither to draw. [4:16] Jesus saith unto her, Go, call thy husband, and come hither.[4:17] The woman answered and said, I have no husband. Jesus said unto her, Thou hast well said, I have no husband:[4:18] For thou hast had five husbands; and he whom thou now hast is not thy husband: in that saidst thou truly. [4:19] The woman saith unto him, Sir, I perceive that thou art a prophet. [4:20] Our fathers worshipped in this mountain; and ye say, that in Jerusalem is the place where men ought to worship. [4:21] Jesus saith unto her, Woman, believe me, the hour cometh, when ye shall neither in this mountain, nor yet at Jerusalem, worship the Father. [4:22] Ye worship ye know not what: we know what we worship: for salvation is of the Jews. [4:23] But the hour cometh, and now is, when the true worshippers shall worship the Father in spirit and in truth: for the Father seeketh such to worship him. [4:24] God [is] a Spirit: and they that worship him must worship [him] in spirit and in truth. [4:25] The woman saith unto him, I know that Messias cometh, which is called Christ: when he is come, he will tell us all things.[4:26] Jesus saith unto her, I that speak unto thee am [he][4:27] And upon this came his disciples, and marvelled that he talked with the woman: yet no man said, What seekest thou? or, Why talkest thou with her? [4:28] The woman then left her waterpot, and went her way into the city, and saith to the men, [4:29] Come, see a man, which told me all things that ever I did: is not this the Christ?[4:30] Then they went out of the city, and came unto him.

[4:31] In the mean while his disciples prayed him, saying, Master, eat. [4:32] But he said unto them, I have meat to eat that ye know not of. [4:33] Therefore said the disciples one to another, Hath any man brought him [ought] to eat? [4:34] Jesus saith unto them, My meat is to do the will of him that sent me, and to finish his work. [4:35] Say not ye, There are yet four months, and [then] cometh harvest? behold, I say unto you, Lift up your eyes, and look on the fields; for they are white already to harvest. [4:36] And he that reapeth receiveth wages, and gathereth fruit unto life eternal: that both he that soweth and he that reapeth may rejoice together. [4:37] And herein is that saying true, One soweth, and another reapeth. [4:38] I sent you to reap that whereon ye bestowed no labour: other men laboured, and ye are entered into their labours.

[4:39] And many of the Samaritans of that city believed on him for the saying of the woman, which testified, He told me all that ever I did. [4:40] So when the Samaritans were come unto him, they besought him that he would tarry with them: and he abode there two days. [4:41] And many more believed because of his own word; [4:42] And said unto the woman, Now we believe, not because of thy saying: for we have heard [him] ourselves, and know that this is indeed the Christ, the Saviour of the world.

[4:43] Now after two days he departed thence, and went into Galilee. [4:44] For Jesus himself testified, that a prophet hath no honour in his own country. [4:45] Then when he was come into Galilee, the Galilaeans received him, having seen all the things that he did at Jerusalem at the feast: for they also went unto the feast. [4:46] So Jesus came again into Cana of Galilee, where he made the water wine. And there was a certain nobleman, whose son was sick at Capernaum. [4:47] When he heard that Jesus was come out of Judaea into Galilee, he went unto him, and besought him that he would come down, and heal his son: for he was at the point of death. [4:48] Then said Jesus unto him, Except ye see signs and wonders, ye will not believe.[4:49] The nobleman saith unto him, Sir, come down ere my child die. [4:50] Jesus saith unto him, Go thy way; thy son liveth. And the man believed the word that Jesus had spoken unto him, and he went his way. [4:51] And as he was now going down, his servants met him, and told [him,] saying, Thy son liveth. [4:52] Then enquired he of them the hour when he began to amend. And they said unto him, Yesterday at the seventh hour the fever left him. [4:53] So the father knew that [it was] at the same hour, in the which Jesus said unto him, Thy son liveth: and himself believed, and his whole house. [4:54] This [is] again the second miracle [that] Jesus did, when he was come out of Judaea into Galilee.

Chapter 5

[5:1] After this there was a feast of the Jews; and Jesus went up to Jerusalem. [5:2] Now there is at Jerusalem by the sheep [market] a pool, which is called in the Hebrew tongue Bethesda, having five porches. [5:3] In these lay a great multitude of impotent folk, of blind, halt, withered, waiting for the moving of the water. [5:4] For an angel went down at a certain season into the pool, and troubled the water: whosoever then first after the troubling of the water stepped in was made whole of whatsoever disease he had. [5:5] And a certain man was there, which had an infirmity thirty and eight years. [5:6] When Jesus saw him lie, and knew that he had been now a long time [in that case,] he saith unto him, Wilt thou be made whole? [5:7] The impotent man answered him, Sir, I have no man, when the water is troubled, to put me into the pool: but while I am coming, another steppeth down before me. [5:8] Jesus saith unto him, Rise, take up thy bed, and walk. [5:9] And immediately the man was made whole, and took up his bed, and walked: and on the same day was the sabbath.

[5:10] The Jews therefore said unto him that was cured, It is the sabbath day: it is not lawful for thee to carry [thy] bed. [5:11] He answered them, He that made me whole, the same said unto me, Take up thy bed, and walk. [5:12] Then asked they him, What man is that which said unto thee, Take up thy bed, and walk? [5:13] And he that was healed wist not who it was: for Jesus had conveyed himself away, a multitude being in [that] place. [5:14] Afterward Jesus findeth him in the temple, and said unto him, Behold, thou art made whole: sin no more, lest a worse thing come unto thee. [5:15] The man departed, and told the Jews that it was Jesus, which had made him whole. [5:16] And therefore did the Jews persecute Jesus, and sought to slay him, because he had done these things on the sabbath day.

[5:17] But Jesus answered them, My Father worketh hitherto, and I work. [5:18] Therefore the Jews sought the more to kill him, because he not only had broken the sabbath, but said also that God was his Father, making himself equal with God. [5:19] Then answered Jesus and said unto them, Verily, verily, I say unto you, The Son can do nothing of himself, but what he seeth the Father do: for what things soever he doeth, these also doeth the Son likewise. [5:20] For the Father loveth the Son, and sheweth him all things that himself doeth: and he will shew him greater works than these, that ye may marvel. [5:21] For as the Father raiseth up the dead, and quickeneth [them;] even so the Son quickeneth whom he will. [5:22] For the Father judgeth no man, but hath committed all judgment unto the Son: [5:23] That all [men] should honour the Son, even as they honour the Father. He that honoureth not the Son honoureth not the Father which hath sent him. [5:24] Verily, verily, I say unto you, He that heareth my word, and believeth on him that sent me, hath everlasting life, and shall not come into condemnation; but is passed from death unto life. [5:25] Verily, verily, I say unto you, The hour is coming, and now is, when the dead shall hear the voice of the Son of God: and they that hear shall live. [5:26] For as the Father hath life in himself; so hath he given to the Son to have life in himself; [5:27] And hath given him authority to execute judgment also, because he is the Son of man.[5:28] Marvel not at this: for the hour is coming, in the which all that are in the graves shall hear his voice, [5:29] And shall come forth; they that have done good, unto the resurrection of life; and they that have done evil, unto the resurrection of damnation. [5:30] I can of mine own self do nothing: as I hear, I judge: and my judgment is just; because I seek not mine own will, but the will of the Father which hath sent me. [5:31] If I bear witness of myself, my witness is not true.

[5:32] There is another that beareth witness of me; and I know that the witness which he witnesseth of me is true.[5:33] Ye sent unto John, and he bare witness unto the truth. [5:34] But I receive not testimony from man: but these things I say, that ye might be saved. [5:35] He was a burning and a shining light: and ye were willing for a season to rejoice in his light.

[5:36] But I have greater witness than [that] of John: for the works which the Father hath given me to finish, the same works that I do, bear witness of me, that the Father hath sent me. [5:37] And the Father himself, which hath sent me, hath borne witness of me. Ye have neither heard his voice at any time, nor seen his shape.

[5:38] And ye have not his word abiding in you: for whom he hath sent, him ye believe not.

[5:39] Search the scriptures; for in them ye think ye have eternal life: and they are they which testify of me. [5:40] And ye will not come to me, that ye might have life. [5:41] I receive not honour from men. [5:42] But I know you, that ye have not the love of God in you. [5:43] I am come in my Father's name, and ye receive me not: if another shall come in his own name, him ye will receive. [5:44] How can ye believe, which receive honour one of another, and seek not the honour that [cometh] from God only? [5:45] Do not think that I will accuse you to the Father: there is [one] that accuseth you, [even] Moses, in whom ye trust. [5:46] For had ye believed Moses, ye would have believed me: for he wrote of me. [5:47] But if ye believe not his writings, how shall ye believe my words?

Chapter 6

[6:1] After these things Jesus went over the sea of Galilee, which is [the sea] of Tiberias. [6:2] And a great multitude followed him, because they saw his miracles which he did on them that were diseased. [6:3] And Jesus went up into a mountain, and there he sat with his disciples.[6:4] And the passover, a feast of the Jews, was nigh.

[6:5] When Jesus then lifted up [his] eyes, and saw a great company come unto him, he saith unto Philip, Whence shall we buy bread, that these may eat? [6:6]

And this he said to prove him: for he himself knew what he would do.[6:7] Philip answered him, Two hundred pennyworth of bread is not sufficient for them, that every one of them may take a little. [6:8] One of his disciples, Andrew, Simon Peter's brother, saith unto him, [6:9] There is a lad here, which hath five barley loaves, and two small fishes: but what are they among so many? [6:10] And Jesus said, Make the men sit down. Now there was much grass in the place. So the men sat down, in number about five thousand.[6:11] And Jesus took the loaves; and when he had given thanks, he distributed to the disciples, and the disciples to them that were set down; and likewise of the fishes as much as they would. [6:12] When they were filled, he said unto his disciples, Gather up the fragments that remain, that nothing be lost. [6:13] Therefore they gathered [them] together, and filled twelve baskets with the fragments of the five barley loaves, which remained over and above unto them that had eaten. [6:14] Then those men, when they had seen the miracle that Jesus did, said, This is of a truth that prophet that should come into the world.

[6:15] When Jesus therefore perceived that they would come and take him by force, to make him a king, he departed again into a mountain himself alone. [6:16] And when even was [now] come, his disciples went down unto the sea, [6:17] And entered into a ship, and went over the sea toward Capernaum. And it was now dark, and Jesus was not come to them. [6:18] And the sea arose by reason of a great wind that blew. [6:19] So when they had rowed about five and twenty or thirty furlongs, they see Jesus walking on the sea, and drawing nigh unto the ship: and they were afraid. [6:20] But he saith unto them, It is I; be not afraid.[6:21] Then they willingly received him into the ship: and immediately the ship was at the land whither they went.

[6:22] The day following, when the people which stood on the other side of the sea saw that there was none other boat there, save that one whereinto his disciples were entered, and that Jesus went not with his disciples into the boat, but [that] his disciples were gone away alone; [6:23](Howbeit there came other boats from Tiberias nigh unto the place where they did eat bread, after that the Lord had given thanks:) [6:24] When the people therefore saw that Jesus was not there, neither his disciples, they also took shipping, and came to Capernaum, seeking for Jesus. [6:25] And when they had found him on the other side of the sea, they said unto him, Rabbi, when camest thou hither? [6:26] Jesus answered them and said, Verily, verily, I say unto you, Ye seek me, not because ye saw the miracles, but because ye did eat of the loaves, and were filled. [6:27] Labour not for the meat which perisheth, but for that meat which endureth unto everlasting life, which the Son of man shall give unto you: for him hath God the Father sealed.[6:28] Then said they unto him, What shall we do, that we might work the works of God? [6:29] Jesus answered and said unto them, This is the work of God, that ye believe on him whom he hath sent. [6:30] They said therefore unto him, What sign shewest thou then, that we may see, and believe thee? what dost thou work? [6:31] Our fathers did eat manna in the desert; as it is written, He gave them bread from heaven to eat. [6:32] Then Jesus said unto them, Verily, verily, I say unto you, Moses gave you not that bread from heaven; but my Father giveth you the true bread from heaven. [6:33] For the bread of God is he which cometh down from heaven, and giveth life unto the world.[6:34] Then said they unto him, Lord, evermore give us this bread. [6:35] And Jesus said unto them, I am the bread of life: he that cometh to me shall never hunger; and he that believeth on me shall never thirst. [6:36] But I said unto you, That ye also have seen me, and believe not. [6:37] All that the Father giveth me shall come to me; and him that cometh to me I will in no wise cast out. [6:38] For I came down from heaven, not to do mine own will, but the will of him that sent me. [6:39] And this is the Father's will which hath sent me, that of all which he hath given me I should lose nothing, but should raise it up again at the last day.[6:40] And this is the will of him that sent me, that everyone which seeth the Son, and believeth on him, may have everlasting life: and I will raise him up at the last day.[6:41] The Jews then murmured at him, because he said, I am the bread which came down from heaven. [6:42] And they said, Is not this Jesus, the son of Joseph, whose father and mother we know? how is it then that he saith, I came down from heaven? [6:43] Jesus therefore answered and said unto them, Murmur not among yourselves. [6:44] No man can come to me, except the Father which hath sent me draw him: and I will raise him up at the last day. [6:45] It is written in the prophets, And they shall be all taught of God. Every man therefore that hath heard, and hath learned of the Father, cometh unto me. [6:46] Not that any man hath seen the Father, save he which is of God, he hath seen the Father.[6:47] Verily, verily, I say unto you, He that believeth on me hath everlasting life. [6:48] I am that bread of life.[6:49] Your fathers did eat manna in the wilderness, and are dead. [6:50] This is the bread which cometh down from heaven, that a man may eat thereof, and not die. [6:51] I am the living bread which came down from heaven: if any man eat of this bread, he shall live forever: and the bread that I will give is my flesh, which I will give for the life of the world. [6:52] The Jews therefore strove among themselves, saying, How can this man give us [his] flesh to eat? [6:53] Then Jesus said unto them, Verily, verily, I say unto you, Except ye eat the flesh of the Son of man, and drink his blood, ye have no life in you. [6:54] Whoso eateth my flesh, and drinketh my blood, hath eternal life; and I will raise him up at the last day. [6:55] For my flesh is meat indeed, and my blood is drink indeed. [6:56] He that eateth my flesh, and drinketh my blood, dwelleth in me, and I in him. [6:57] As the living Father hath sent me, and I live by the Father: so he that eateth me, even he shall live by me.[6:58] This is that bread which came down from heaven: not as your fathers did eat manna, and are dead: he that eateth of this bread shall live forever. [6:59] These things said he in the synagogue, as he taught in Capernaum.[6:60] Many therefore of his disciples, when they had heard [this,] said, This is an hard saying; who can hear it?[6:61] When Jesus knew in himself that his disciples murmured at it, he said unto them, Doth this offend you?[6:62] [What] and if ye shall see the Son of man ascend up where he was before? [6:63] It is the spirit that quickeneth; the flesh profiteth nothing: the words that I speak unto you,[they] are spirit, and [they] are life. [6:64] But there are some of you that believe not. For Jesus knew from the beginning who they were that believed not, and who should betray him. [6:65] And he said, Therefore said I unto you, that no man can come unto me, except it were given unto him of my Father.

[6:66] From that [time] many of his disciples went back, and walked no more with him. [6:67] Then said Jesus unto the twelve, Will ye also go away? [6:68] Then Simon Peter answered him, Lord, to whom shall we go? thou hast the words of eternal life. [6:69] And we believe and are sure that thou art that Christ, the Son of the living God. [6:70] Jesus answered them, Have not I chosen you twelve, and one of you is a devil? [6:71] He spake of Judas Iscariot [the son] of Simon: for he it was that should betray him, being one of the twelve.

Chapter 7

[7:1] After these things Jesus walked in Galilee: for he would not walk in Jewry, because the Jews sought to kill him. [7:2] Now the Jews' feast of tabernacles was at hand. [7:3] His brethren therefore said unto him, Depart hence, and go into Judaea, that thy disciples also may see the works that thou doest. [7:4] For [there is] no man [that] doeth anything in secret, and he himself seeketh to be known openly. If thou do these things, shew thyself to the world. [7:5] For neither did his brethren believe in him.[7:6] Then Jesus said unto them, My time is not yet come: but your time is alway ready. [7:7] The world cannot hate you; but me it hateth, because I testify of it, that the works thereof are evil. [7:8] Go ye up unto this feast: I go not up yet unto this feast; for my time is not yet full come. [7:9] When he had said these words unto them, he abode [still] in Galilee.

[7:10] But when his brethren were gone up, then went he also up unto the feast, not openly, but as it were in secret.[7:11] Then the Jews sought him at the feast, and said, Where is he? [7:12] And there was much murmuring among the people concerning him: for some said, He is a good man: others said, Nay; but he deceiveth the people.[7:13] Howbeit no man spake openly of him for fear of the Jews.

[7:14] Now about the midst of the feast Jesus went up into the temple, and taught. [7:15] And the Jews marvelled, saying, How knoweth this man letters, having never learned? [7:16] Jesus answered them, and said, My doctrine is not mine, but his that sent me. [7:17] If any man will do his will, he shall know of the doctrine, whether it be of God, or [whether] I speak of myself. [7:18] He that speaketh of himself seeketh his own glory: but he that seeketh his glory that sent him, the same is true, and no unrighteousness is in him. [7:19] Did not Moses give you the law, and [yet] none of you keepeth the law? Why go ye about to kill me? [7:20] The people answered and said, Thou hast a devil: who goeth about to kill thee? [7:21] Jesus answered and said unto them, I have done one work, and ye all marvel. [7:22] Moses therefore gave unto you circumcision; (not because it is of Moses, but of the fathers;) and ye on the sabbath day circumcise a man.[7:23] If a man on the sabbath day receive circumcision, that the law of Moses should not be broken; are ye angry at me, because I have made a man every whit whole on the sabbath day? [7:24] Judge not according to the appearance, but judge righteous judgment. [7:25] Then said some of them of Jerusalem, Is not this he, whom they seek to kill?[7:26] But, lo, he speaketh boldly, and they say nothing unto him. Do the rulers know indeed that this is the very Christ? [7:27] Howbeit we know this man whence he is: but when Christ cometh, no man knoweth whence he is.[7:28] Then cried Jesus in the temple as he taught, saying, Ye both know me, and ye know whence I am: and I am not come of myself, but he that sent me is true, whom ye know not. [7:29] But I know him: for I am from him, and he hath sent me. [7:30] Then they sought to take him: but no man laid hands on him, because his hour was not yet come.[7:31] And many of the people believed on him, and said, When Christ cometh, will he do more miracles than these which this [man] hath done?

[7:32] The Pharisees heard that the people murmured such things concerning him; and the Pharisees and the chief priests sent officers to take him. [7:33] Then said Jesus unto them, Yet a little while am I with you, and [then] I go unto him that sent me. [7:34] Ye shall seek me, and shall not find [me:] and where I am, [thither] ye cannot come.[7:35] Then said the Jews among themselves, Whither will he go, that we shall not find him? will he go unto the dispersed among the Gentiles, and teach the Gentiles? [7:36] What [manner of] saying is this that he said, Ye shall seek me, and shall not find [me:] and where I am,[thither] ye cannot come? [7:37] In the last day, that great [day] of the feast, Jesus stood and cried, saying, If any man thirst, let him come unto me, and drink. [7:38] He that believeth on me, as the scripture hath said, out of his belly shall flow rivers of living water. [7:39] (But this spake he of the Spirit, which they that believe on him should receive: for the Holy Ghost was not yet [given;] because that Jesus was not yet glorified.)

[7:40] Many of the people therefore, when they heard this saying, said, Of a truth this is the Prophet. [7:41] Others said, This is the Christ. But some said, Shall Christ come out of Galilee? [7:42] Hath not the scripture said, That Christ cometh of the seed of David, and out of the town of Bethlehem, where David was? [7:43] So there was a division among the people because of him. [7:44] And some of them would have taken him; but no man laid hands on him.

[7:45] Then came the officers to the chief priests and Pharisees; and they said unto them, Why have ye not brought him? [7:46] The officers answered, Never man spake like this man. [7:47] Then answered them the Pharisees, Are ye also deceived? [7:48] Have any of the rulers or of the Pharisees believed on him? [7:49] But this people who knoweth not the law are cursed. [7:50]

Nicodemus saith unto them, (he that came to Jesus by night, being one of them,) [7:51] Doth our law judge [any] man, before it hear him, and know what he doeth? [7:52] They answered and said unto him, Art thou also of Galilee? Search, and look: for out of Galilee ariseth no prophet.[7:53] And every man went unto his own house.

Chapter 8

[8:1] Jesus went unto the mount of Olives. [8:2] And early in the morning he came again into the temple, and all the people came unto him; and he sat down, and taught them. [8:3] And the scribes and Pharisees brought unto him a woman taken in adultery; and when they had set her in the midst, [8:4] They say unto him, Master, this woman was taken in adultery, in the very act. [8:5] Now Moses in the law commanded us, that such should be stoned: but what sayest thou? [8:6] This they said, tempting him, that they might have to accuse him. But Jesus stooped down, and with [his] finger wrote on the ground, [as though he heard them not.][8:7] So when they continued asking him, he lifted up himself, and said unto them, He that is without sin among you, let him first cast a stone at her. [8:8] And again he stooped down, and wrote on the ground. [8:9] And they which heard [it,] being convicted by [their own] conscience, went out one by one, beginning at the eldest, [even] unto the last: and Jesus was left alone, and the woman standing in the midst. [8:10] When Jesus had lifted up himself, and saw none but the woman, he said unto her, Woman, where are those thine accusers? hath no man condemned thee?[8:11] She said, No man, Lord. And Jesus said unto her, Neither do I condemn thee: go, and sin no more.

[8:12] Then spake Jesus again unto them, saying, I am the light of the world: he that followeth me shall not walk in darkness, but shall have the light of life. [8:13] The Pharisees therefore said unto him, Thou bearest record of thyself; thy record is not true. [8:14] Jesus answered and said unto them, Though I bear record of myself, [yet] my record is true: for I know whence I came, and whither I go; but ye cannot tell whence I come, and whither I go. [8:15] Ye judge after the flesh; I judge no man. [8:16] And yet if I judge, my judgment is true: for I am not alone, but I and the Father that sent me. [8:17] It is also written in your law, that the testimony of two men is true. [8:18] I am one that bear witness of myself, and the Father that sent me beareth witness of me. [8:19] Then said they unto him, Where is thy Father? Jesus answered, Ye neither know me, nor my Father: if ye had known me, ye should have known my Father also. [8:20] These words spake Jesus in the treasury, as he taught in the temple: and no man laid hands on him; for his hour was not yet come. [8:21] Then said Jesus again unto them, I go my way, and ye shall seek me, and shall die in your sins: whither I go, ye cannot come. [8:22] Then said the Jews, Will he kill himself? because he saith, Whither I go, ye cannot come. [8:23] And he said unto them, Ye are from beneath; I am from above: ye are of this world; I am not of this world. [8:24] I said therefore unto you, that ye shall die in your sins: for if ye believe not that I am [he,] ye shall die in your sins. [8:25] Then said they unto him, Who art thou? And Jesus saith unto them, Even [the same] that I said unto you from the beginning. [8:26] I have many things to say and to judge of you: but he that sent me is true; and I speak to the world those things which I have heard of him. [8:27] They understood not that he spake to them of the Father. [8:28] Then said Jesus unto them, When ye have lifted up the Son of man, then shall ye know that I am [he,] and [that] I do nothing of myself; but as my Father hath taught me, I speak these things. [8:29] And he that sent me is with me: the Father hath not left me alone; for I do always those things that please him. [8:30] As he spake these words, many believed on him. [8:31] Then said Jesus to those Jews which believed on him, If ye continue in my word, [then] are ye my disciples indeed;[8:32] And ye shall know the truth, and the truth shall make you free.

[8:33] They answered him, We be Abraham's seed, and were never in bondage to any man: how sayest thou, Ye shall be made free? [8:34] Jesus answered them, Verily, verily, I say unto you, Whosoever committeth sin is the servant of sin. [8:35] And the servant abideth not in the house for ever: [but] the Son abideth ever. [8:36] If the Son therefore shall make you free, ye shall be free indeed.[8:37] I know that ye are Abraham's seed; but ye seek to kill me, because my word hath no place in you. [8:38] I speak that which I have seen with my Father: and ye do that which ye have seen with your father. [8:39] They answered and said unto him, Abraham is our father. Jesus saith unto them, If ye were Abraham's children, ye would do the works of Abraham. [8:40] But now ye seek to kill me, a man that hath told you the truth, which I have heard of God: this did not Abraham. [8:41] Ye do the deeds of your father. Then said they to him, We be not born of fornication; we have one Father, [even] God. [8:42] Jesus said unto them, If God were your Father, ye would love me: for I proceeded forth and came from God; neither came I of myself, but he sent me. [8:43] Why do ye not understand my speech? [even] because ye cannot hear my word. [8:44] Ye are of your father the devil, and the lusts of [your] father ye will do. He was a murderer from the beginning, and abode not in the truth, because there is no truth in him. When he speaketh a lie, he speaketh of his own: for he is a liar, and the father of it. [8:45] And because I tell [you] the truth, ye believe me not. [8:46] Which of you convinceth me of sin? And if I say the truth, why do ye not believe me?[8:47] He that is of God heareth God's words: ye therefore hear [them] not, because ye are not of God. [8:48] Then answered the Jews, and said unto him, Say we not well that thou art a Samaritan, and hast a devil? [8:49] Jesus answered, I have not a devil; but I honour my Father, and ye do dishonour me. [8:50] And I seek not mine own glory: there is one that seeketh and judgeth. [8:51] Verily, verily, I say unto you, If a man keep my saying, he shall never see death. [8:52] Then said the Jews unto him, Now we know that thou hast a devil. Abraham is dead, and the prophets; and thou sayest, If a man keep my saying, he shall never taste of death. [8:53] Art thou greater than our father Abraham, which is dead? and the prophets are dead: whom makest thou thyself? [8:54] Jesus answered, If I honour myself, my honour is nothing: it is my Father that honoureth me; of whom ye say, that he is your God: [8:55] Yet ye have not known him; but I know him: and if I should say, I know him not, I shall be a liar like unto you: but I know him, and keep his saying. [8:56] Your father Abraham rejoiced to see my day: and he saw [it,] and was glad.[8:57] Then said the Jews unto him, Thou art not yet fifty years old, and hast thou seen Abraham? [8:58] Jesus said unto them, Verily, verily, I say unto you, Before Abraham was, I am. [8:59] Then took they up stones to cast at him: but Jesus hid himself, and went out of the temple, going through the midst of them, and so passed by.

Chapter 9

[9:1] And as [Jesus] passed by, he saw a man which was blind from [his] birth. [9:2] And his disciples asked him, saying, Master, who did sin, this man, or his parents, that he was born blind? [9:3] Jesus answered, Neither hath this man sinned, nor his parents: but that the works of God should be made manifest in him. [9:4] I must work the works of him that sent me, while it is day: the night cometh, when no man can work. [9:5] As long as I am in the world, I am the light of the world. [9:6] When he had thus spoken, he spat on the ground, and made clay of the spittle, and he anointed the eyes of the blind man with the clay, [9:7] And said unto him, Go, wash in the pool of Siloam, (which is by interpretation, Sent.) [9:8] The neighbours therefore, and they which before had seen him that he was blind, said, Is not this he that sat and begged? [9:9] Some said, This is he: others [said,] He is like him: [but] he said, I am [he.][9:10] Therefore said they unto him, How were thine eyes opened? [9:11] He answered and said, A man that is called Jesus made clay, and anointed mine eyes, and said unto me, Go to the pool of Siloam, and wash: and I went and washed, and I received sight. [9:12] Then said they unto him, Where is he? He said, I know not.

[9:13] They brought to the Pharisees him that aforetime was blind. [9:14] And it was the sabbath day when Jesus made the clay, and opened his eyes. [9:15] Then again the Pharisees also asked him how he had received his sight. He said unto them, He put clay upon mine eyes, and I washed, and do see. [9:16] Therefore said some of the Pharisees, This man is not of God, because he keepeth not the sabbath day. Others said, How can a man that is a sinner do such miracles? And there was a division among them. [9:17] They say unto the blind man again, What sayest thou of him, that he hath opened thine eyes? He said, He is a prophet. [9:18] But the Jews did not believe concerning him, that he had been blind, and received his sight, until they called the parents of him that had received his sight.[9:19] And they asked them, saying, Is this your son, who ye say was born blind? how then doth he now see? [9:20] His parents answered them and said, We know that this is our son, and that he was born blind: [9:21] But by what means he now seeth, we know not; or who hath opened his eyes, we know not: he is of age; ask him: he shall speak for himself. [9:22] These [words] spake his parents, because they feared the Jews: for the Jews had agreed already, that if any man did confess that he was Christ, he should be put out of the synagogue. [9:23] Therefore said his parents, He is of age; ask him. [9:24] Then again called they the man that was blind, and said unto him, Give God the praise: we know that this man is a sinner. [9:25] He answered and said, Whether he be a sinner [or no,] I know not: one thing I know, that, whereas I was blind, now I see. [9:26] Then said they to him again, What did he to thee? how opened he thine eyes? [9:27] He answered them, I have told you already, and ye did not hear: wherefore would ye hear [it] again? will ye also be his disciples? [9:28] Then they reviled him, and said, Thou art his disciple; but we are Moses' disciples. [9:29] We know that God spake unto Moses: [as for] this [fellow,] we know not from whence he is. [9:30] The man answered and said unto them, Why herein is a marvellous thing, that ye know not from whence he is, and [yet] he hath opened mine eyes. [9:31] Now we know that God heareth not sinners: but if any man be a worshipper of God, and doeth his will, him he heareth.[9:32] Since the world began was it not heard that any man opened the eyes of one that was born blind. [9:33] If this man were not of God, he could do nothing. [9:34] They answered and said unto him, Thou wast altogether born in sins, and dost thou teach us? And they cast him out. [9:35] Jesus heard that they had cast him out; and when he had found him, he said unto him, Dost thou believe on the Son of God? [9:36] He answered and said, Who is he, Lord, that I might believe on him? [9:37] And Jesus said unto him, Thou hast both seen him, and it is he that talketh with thee. [9:38] And he said, Lord, I believe. And he worshipped him.

[9:39] And Jesus said, For judgment I am come into this world, that they which see not might see; and that they which see might be made blind. [9:40] And [some] of the Pharisees which were with him heard these words, and said unto him, Are we blind also? [9:41] Jesus said unto them, If ye were blind, ye should have no sin: but now ye say, We see; therefore your sin remaineth.

Chapter 10

[10:1] Verily, verily, I say unto you, He that entereth not by the door into the sheepfold, but climbeth up some other way, the same is a thief and a robber. [10:2] But he that entereth in by the door is the shepherd of the sheep. [10:3] To him the porter openeth; and the sheep hear his voice: and he calleth his own sheep by name, and leadeth them out.[10:4] And when he putteth forth his own sheep, he goeth before them, and the sheep follow him: for they know his voice. [10:5] And a stranger will they not follow, but will flee from him: for they know not the voice of strangers.[10:6] This parable spake Jesus unto them: but they understood not what things they were which he spake unto them. [10:7] Then said Jesus unto them again, Verily, verily, I say unto you, I am the door of the sheep. [10:8] All that ever came before me are thieves and robbers: but the sheep did not hear them. [10:9] I am the door: by me if any man enter in, he shall be saved, and shall go in and out, and find pasture. [10:10] The thief cometh not, but for to steal, and to kill, and to destroy: I am come that they might have life, and that they might have [it] more abundantly.[10:11] I am the good shepherd: the good shepherd giveth his life for the sheep. [10:12] But he that is an hireling, and not the shepherd, whose own the sheep are not, seeth the wolf coming, and leaveth the sheep, and fleeth: and the wolf catcheth them, and scattereth the sheep. [10:13] The hireling fleeth, because he is an hireling, and careth not for the sheep. [10:14] I am the good shepherd, and know my [sheep,] and am known of mine. [10:15] As the Father knoweth me, even so know I the Father: and I lay down my life for the sheep. [10:16] And other sheep I have, which are not of this fold: them also I must bring, and they shall hear my voice; and there shall be one fold, [and] one shepherd. [10:17] Therefore doth my Father love me, because I lay down my life, that I might take it again.[10:18] No man taketh it from me, but I lay it down of myself. I have power to lay it down, and I have power to take it again. This commandment have I received of my Father.

[10:19] There was a division therefore again among the Jews for these sayings. [10:20] And many of them said, He hath a devil, and is mad; why hear ye him? [10:21] Others said, These are not the words of him that hath a devil. Can a devil open the eyes of the blind?

[10:22] And it was at Jerusalem the feast of the dedication, and it was winter. [10:23] And Jesus walked in the temple in Solomon's porch. [10:24] Then came the Jews round about him, and said unto him, How long dost thou make us to doubt? If thou be the Christ, tell us plainly.[10:25] Jesus answered them, I told you, and ye believed not: the works that I do in my Father's name, they bear witness of me. [10:26] But ye believe not, because ye are not of my sheep, as I said unto you. [10:27] My sheep hear my voice, and I know them, and they follow me: [10:28] And I give unto them eternal life; and they shall never perish, neither shall any [man] pluck them out of my hand.[10:29] My Father, which gave [them] me, is greater than all; and no [man] is able to pluck [them] out of my Father's hand. [10:30] I and [my] Father are one. [10:31] Then the Jews took up stones again to stone him. [10:32] Jesus answered them, Many good works have I shewed you from my Father; for which of those works do ye stone me?[10:33] The Jews answered him, saying, For a good work we stone thee not; but for blasphemy; and because that thou, being a man, makest thyself God. [10:34] Jesus answered them, Is it not written in your law, I said, Ye are gods?[10:35] If he called them gods, unto whom the word of God came, and the scripture cannot be broken; [10:36] Say ye of him, whom the Father hath sanctified, and sent into the world, Thou blasphemest; because I said, I am the Son of God? [10:37] If I do not the works of my Father, believe me not. [10:38] But if I do, though ye believe not me, believe the works: that ye may know, and believe, that the Father is in me, and I in him. [10:39] Therefore they sought again to take him: but he escaped out of their hand, [10:40] And went away again beyond Jordan into the place where John at first baptized; and there he abode. [10:41] And many resorted unto him, and said, John did no miracle: but all things that John spake of this man were true. [10:42] And many believed on him there.

Chapter 11

[11:1] Now a certain [man] was sick, [named] Lazarus, of Bethany, the town of Mary and her sister Martha. [11:2](It was [that] Mary which anointed the Lord with ointment, and wiped his feet with her hair, whose brother Lazarus was sick.) [11:3] Therefore his sisters sent unto him, saying, Lord, behold, he whom thou lovest is sick. [11:4] When Jesus heard [that,] he said, This sickness is not unto death, but for the glory of God, that the Son of God might be glorified thereby. [11:5] Now Jesus loved Martha, and her sister, and Lazarus. [11:6] When he had heard therefore that he was sick, he abode two days still in the same place where he was. [11:7] Then after that saith he to [his] disciples, Let us go into Judaea again. [11:8] [His] disciples say unto him, Master, the Jews of late sought to stone thee; and goest thou thither again? [11:9] Jesus answered, Are there not twelve hours in the day? If any man walk in the day, he stumbleth not, because he seeth the light of this world. [11:10] But if a man walk in the night, he stumbleth, because there is no light in him. [11:11] These things said he: and after that he saith unto them, Our friend Lazarus sleepeth; but I go, that I may awake him out of sleep.[11:12] Then said his disciples, Lord, if he sleep, he shall do well. [11:13] Howbeit Jesus spake of his death: but they thought that he had spoken of taking of rest in sleep.[11:14] Then said Jesus unto them plainly, Lazarus is dead.[11:15] And I am glad for your sakes that I was not there, to the intent ye may believe; nevertheless let us go unto him. [11:16] Then said Thomas, which is called Didymus, unto his fellowdisciples, Let us also go, that we may die with him. [11:17] Then when Jesus came, he found that he had [lain] in the grave four days already. [11:18] Now Bethany was nigh unto Jerusalem, about fifteen furlongs off: [11:19] And many of the Jews came to Martha and Mary, to comfort them concerning their brother. [11:20] Then Martha, as soon as she heard that Jesus was coming, went and met him: but Mary sat [still] in the house. [11:21] Then said Martha unto Jesus, Lord, if thou hadst been here, my brother had not died. [11:22] But I know, that even now, whatsoever thou wilt ask of God, God will give [it] thee. [11:23] Jesus saith unto her, Thy brother shall rise again. [11:24] Martha saith unto him, I know that he shall rise again in the resurrection at the last day. [11:25] Jesus said unto her, I am the resurrection, and the life: he that believeth in me, though he were dead, yet shall he live:[11:26] And whosoever liveth and believeth in me shall never die. Believest thou this? [11:27] She saith unto him, Yea, Lord: I believe that thou art the Christ, the Son of God, which should come into the world. [11:28] And when she had so said, she went her way, and called Mary her sister secretly, saying, The Master is come, and calleth for thee.[11:29] As soon as she heard [that,] she arose quickly, and came unto him. [11:30] Now Jesus was not yet come into the town, but was in that place where Martha met him.[11:31] The Jews then which were with her in the house, and comforted her, when they saw Mary, that she rose up hastily and went out, followed her, saying, She goeth unto the grave to weep there. [11:32] Then when Mary was come where Jesus was, and saw him, she fell down at his feet, saying unto him, Lord, if thou hadst been here, my brother had not died. [11:33] When Jesus therefore saw her weeping, and the Jews also weeping which came with her, he groaned in the spirit, and was troubled, [11:34] And said, Where have ye laid him? They said unto him, Lord, come and see. [11:35] Jesus wept. [11:36] Then said the Jews, Behold how he loved him! [11:37] And some of them said, Could not this man, which opened the eyes of the blind, have caused that even this man should not have died?[11:38] Jesus therefore again groaning in himself cometh to the grave. It was a cave, and a stone lay upon it. [11:39] Jesus said, Take ye away the stone. Martha, the sister of him that was dead, saith unto him, Lord, by this time he stinketh: for he hath been [dead] four days. [11:40] Jesus saith unto her, Said I not unto thee, that, if thou wouldest believe, thou shouldest see the glory of God? [11:41] Then they took away the stone [from the place] where the dead was laid. And Jesus lifted up [his] eyes, and said, Father, I thank thee that thou hast heard me. [11:42] And I knew that thou hearest me always: but because of the people which stand by I said [it,] that they may believe that thou hast sent me.[11:43] And when he thus had spoken, he cried with a loud voice, Lazarus, come forth. [11:44] And he that was dead came forth, bound hand and foot with graveclothes: and his face was bound about with a napkin. Jesus saith unto them,

Loose him, and let him go. [11:45] Then many of the Jews which came to Mary, and had seen the things which Jesus did, believed on him. [11:46] But some of them went their ways to the Pharisees, and told them what things Jesus had done.

[11:47] Then gathered the chief priests and the Pharisees a council, and said, What do we? for this man doeth many miracles. [11:48] If we let him thus alone, all [men] will believe on him: and the Romans shall come and take away both our place and nation. [11:49] And one of them,[named] Caiaphas, being the high priest that same year, said unto them, Ye know nothing at all, [11:50] Nor consider that it is expedient for us, that one man should die for the people, and that the whole nation perish not. [11:51] And this spake he not of himself: but being high priest that year, he prophesied that Jesus should die for that nation; [11:52] And not for that nation only, but that also he should gather together in one the children of God that were scattered abroad. [11:53] Then from that day forth they took counsel together for to put him to death. [11:54] Jesus therefore walked no more openly among the Jews; but went thence unto a country near to the wilderness, into a city called Ephraim, and there continued with his disciples.

[11:55] And the Jews' passover was nigh at hand: and many went out of the country up to Jerusalem before the passover, to purify themselves. [11:56] Then sought they for Jesus, and spake among themselves, as they stood in the temple, What think ye, that he will not come to the feast?[11:57] Now both the chief priests and the Pharisees had given a commandment, that, if any man knew where he were, he should shew [it,] that they might take him.

Chapter 12

[12:1] Then Jesus six days before the passover came to Bethany, where Lazarus was which had been dead, whom he raised from the dead. [12:2] There they made him a supper; and Martha served: but Lazarus was one of them that sat at the table with him. [12:3] Then took Mary a pound of ointment of spikenard, very costly, and anointed the feet of Jesus, and wiped his feet with her hair: and the house was filled with the odour of the ointment. [12:4] Then saith one of his disciples, Judas Iscariot, Simon's [son,] which should betray him, [12:5] Why was not this ointment sold for three hundred pence, and given to the poor? [12:6] This he said, not that he cared for the poor; but because he was a thief, and had the bag, and bare what was put therein. [12:7] Then said Jesus, Let her alone: against the day of my burying hath she kept this. [12:8] For the poor always ye have with you; but me ye have not always. [12:9] Much people of the Jews therefore knew that he was there: and they came not for Jesus' sake only, but that they might see Lazarus also, whom he had raised from the dead.

[12:10] But the chief priests consulted that they might put Lazarus also to death; [12:11] Because that by reason of him many of the Jews went away, and believed on Jesus.

[12:12] On the next day much people that were come to the feast, when they heard that Jesus was coming to Jerusalem, [12:13] Took branches of palm trees, and went forth to meet him, and cried, Hosanna: Blessed [is] the King of Israel that cometh in the name of the Lord. [12:14] And Jesus, when he had found a young ass, sat thereon; as it is written, [12:15] Fear not, daughter of Sion: behold, thy King cometh, sitting on an ass's colt. [12:16] These things understood not his disciples at the first: but when Jesus was glorified, then remembered they that these things were written of him, and [that] they had done these things unto him. [12:17] The people therefore that was with him when he called Lazarus out of his grave, and raised him from the dead, bare record. [12:18] For this cause the people also met him, for that they heard that he had done this miracle.[12:19] The Pharisees therefore said among themselves, Perceive ye how ye prevail nothing? behold, the world is gone after him.

[12:20] And there were certain Greeks among them that came up to worship at the feast: [12:21] The same came therefore to Philip, which was of Bethsaida of Galilee, and desired him, saying, Sir, we would see Jesus. [12:22] Philip cometh and telleth Andrew: and again Andrew and Philip tell Jesus.

[12:23] And Jesus answered them, saying, The hour is come, that the Son of man should be glorified. [12:24] Verily, verily, I say unto you, Except a corn of wheat fall into the ground and die, it abideth alone: but if it die, it bringeth forth much fruit. [12:25] He that loveth his life shall lose it; and he that hateth his life in this world shall keep it unto life eternal. [12:26] If any man serve me, let him follow me; and where I am, there shall also my servant be: if any man serve me, him will [my] Father honour.[12:27] Now is my soul troubled; and what shall I say?Father, save me from this hour: but for this cause came I unto this hour. [12:28] Father, glorify thy name. Then came there a voice from heaven, [saying,] I have both glorified [it,] and will glorify [it] again. [12:29] The people therefore, that stood by, and heard [it,] said that it thundered: others said, An angel spake to him. [12:30] Jesus answered and said, This voice came not because of me, but for your sakes. [12:31] Now is the judgment of this world: now shall the prince of this world be cast out.[12:32] And I, if I be lifted up from the earth, will draw all [men] unto me. [12:33] This he said, signifying what death he should die. [12:34] The people answered him, We have heard out of the law that Christ abideth for ever: and how sayest thou, The Son of man must be lifted up? who is this Son of man? [12:35] Then Jesus said unto them, Yet a little while is the light with you. Walk while ye have the light, lest darkness come upon you: for he that walketh in darkness knoweth not whither he goeth. [12:36] While ye have light, believe in the light, that ye may be the children of light. These things spake Jesus, and departed, and did hide himself from them.

[12:37] But though he had done so many miracles before them, yet they believed not on him: [12:38] That the saying of Esaias the prophet might be fulfilled, which he spake, Lord, who hath believed our report? and to whom hath the arm of the Lord been revealed? [12:39] Therefore they could not believe, because that Esaias said again, [12:40] He hath blinded their eyes, and hardened their heart; that they should not see with [their] eyes, nor understand with [their] heart, and be converted, and I should heal them.[12:41] These things said Esaias, when he saw his glory, and spake of him.

[12:42] Nevertheless among the chief rulers also many believed on him; but because of the Pharisees they did not confess [him,] lest they should be put out of the synagogue:[12:43] For they loved the praise of men more than the praise of God.

[12:44] Jesus cried and said, He that believeth on me, believeth not on me, but on him that sent me. [12:45] And he that seeth me seeth him that sent me. [12:46] I am come a light into the world, that whosoever believeth on me should not abide in darkness. [12:47] And if any man hear my words, and believe not, I judge him not: for I came not to judge the world, but to save the world. [12:48] He that rejecteth me, and receiveth not my words, hath one that judgeth him: the word that I have spoken, the same shall judge him in the last day. [12:49] For I have not spoken of myself; but the Father which sent me, he gave me a commandment, what I should say, and what I should speak.[12:50] And I know that his commandment is life everlasting: whatsoever I speak therefore, even as the Father said unto me, so I speak.

Chapter 13

[13:1] Now before the feast of the passover, when Jesus knew that his hour was come that he should depart out of this world unto the Father, having loved his own which were in the world, he loved them unto the end. [13:2] And supper being ended, the devil having now put into the heart of Judas Iscariot, Simon's [son,] to betray him; [13:3] Jesus knowing that the Father had given all things into his hands, and that he was come from God, and went to God; [13:4] He riseth from supper, and laid aside his garments; and took a towel, and girded himself. [13:5] After that he poureth water into a bason, and began to wash the disciples' feet, and to wipe [them] with the towel wherewith he was girded.[13:6] Then cometh he to Simon Peter: and Peter saith unto him, Lord, dost thou wash my feet? [13:7] Jesus answered and said unto him, What I do thou knowest not now; but thou shalt know hereafter. [13:8] Peter saith unto him, Thou shalt never wash my feet. Jesus answered him, If I wash thee not, thou hast no part with me. [13:9] Simon Peter saith unto him, Lord, not my feet only, but also [my] hands and [my] head. [13:10] Jesus saith to him, He that is washed needeth not save to wash [his] feet, but is clean every whit: and ye are clean, but not all. [13:11] For he knew who should betray him; therefore said he, Ye are not all clean. [13:12] So after he had washed their feet, and had taken his garments, and was set down again, he said unto them, Know ye what I have done to you? [13:13] Ye call me Master and Lord: and ye say well; for so I am. [13:14]

If I then, [your] Lord and Master, have washed your feet; ye also ought to wash one another's feet. [13:15] For I have given you an example, that ye should do as I have done to you. [13:16] Verily, verily, I say unto you, The servant is not greater than his lord; neither he that is sent greater than he that sent him. [13:17] If ye know these things, happy are ye if ye do them.

[13:18] I speak not of you all: I know whom I have chosen: but that the scripture may be fulfilled, He that eateth bread with me hath lifted up his heel against me.[13:19] Now I tell you before it come, that, when it is come to pass, ye may believe that I am [he.][13:20] Verily, verily, I say unto you, He that receiveth whomsoever I send receiveth me; and he that receiveth me receiveth him that sent me. [13:21] When Jesus had thus said, he was troubled in spirit, and testified, and said, Verily, verily, I say unto you, that one of you shall betray me. [13:22] Then the disciples looked one on another, doubting of whom he spake. [13:23] Now there was leaning on Jesus' bosom one of his disciples, whom Jesus loved. [13:24] Simon Peter therefore beckoned to him, that he should ask who it should be of whom he spake. [13:25] He then lying on Jesus' breast saith unto him, Lord, who is it? [13:26] Jesus answered, He it is, to whom I shall give a sop, when I have dipped [it.] And when he had dipped the sop, he gave [it] to Judas Iscariot, [the son] of Simon. [13:27] And after the sop Satan entered into him. Then said Jesus unto him, That thou doest, do quickly. [13:28] Now no man at the table knew for what intent he spake this unto him. [13:29] For some [of them] thought, because Judas had the bag, that Jesus had said unto him, Buy [those things] that we have need of against the feast; or, that he should give something to the poor. [13:30] He then having received the sop went immediately out: and it was night.

[13:31] Therefore, when he was gone out, Jesus said, Now is the Son of man glorified, and God is glorified in him. [13:32] If God be glorified in him, God shall also glorify him in himself, and shall straightway glorify him.[13:33] Little children, yet a little while I am with you. Ye shall seek me: and as I said unto the Jews, Whither I go, ye cannot come; so now I say to you. [13:34] A new commandment I give unto you, That ye love one another; as I have loved you, that ye also love one another. [13:35] By this shall all [men] know that ye are my disciples, if ye have love one to another.

[13:36] Simon Peter said unto him, Lord, whither goest thou? Jesus answered him, Whither I go, thou canst not follow me now; but thou shalt follow me afterwards.[13:37] Peter said unto him, Lord, why cannot I follow thee now? I will lay down my life for thy sake. [13:38] Jesus answered him, Wilt thou lay down thy life for my sake? Verily, verily, I say unto thee, The cock shall not crow, till thou hast denied me thrice.

Chapter 14

[14:1] Let not your heart be troubled: ye believe in God, believe also in me. [14:2] In my Father's house are many mansions: if [it were] not so, I would have told you. I go to prepare a place for you. [14:3] And if I go and prepare a place for you, I will come again, and receive you unto myself; that where I am, [there] ye may be also. [14:4] And whither I go ye know, and the way ye know. [14:5] Thomas saith unto him, Lord, we know not whither thou goest; and how can we know the way? [14:6] Jesus saith unto him, I am the way, the truth, and the life: no man cometh unto the Father, but by me. [14:7] If ye had known me, ye should have known my Father also: and from henceforth ye know him, and have seen him. [14:8] Philip saith unto him, Lord, shew us the Father, and it sufficeth us.[14:9] Jesus saith unto him, Have I been so long time with you, and yet hast thou not known me, Philip? he that hath seen me hath seen the Father; and how sayest thou [then,] Shew us the Father? [14:10] Believest thou not that I am in the Father, and the Father in me? the words that I speak unto you I speak not of myself: but the Father that dwelleth in me, he doeth the works. [14:11] Believe me that I [am] in the Father, and the Father in me: or else believe me for the very works' sake. [14:12] Verily, verily, I say unto you, He that believeth on me, the works that I do shall he do also; and greater [works] than these shall he do; because I go unto my Father. [14:13] And whatsoever ye shall ask in my name, that will I do, that the Father may be glorified in the Son. [14:14] If ye shall ask any thing in my name, I will do [it][14:15] If ye love me, keep my commandments. [14:16] And I will pray the Father, and he shall give you another Comforter, that he may abide with you forever; [14:17][Even] the Spirit of truth; whom the world cannot receive, because it seeth him not, neither knoweth him: but ye know him; for he dwelleth with you, and shall be in you. [14:18] I will not leave you comfortless: I will come to you.[14:19] Yet a little while, and the world seeth me no more; but ye see me: because I live, ye shall live also. [14:20] At that day ye shall know that I [am] in my Father, and ye in me, and I in you. [14:21] He that hath my commandments, and keepeth them, he it is that loveth me: and he that loveth me shall be loved of my Father, and I will love him, and not Iscariot, Lord, how is it that thou wilt manifest thyself unto us, and not unto the world? [14:23] Jesus answered and said unto him, If a man love me, he will keep my words: and my Father will love him, and we will come unto him, and make our abode with him. [14:24] He that loveth me not keepeth not my sayings: and the word which ye hear is not mine, but the Father's which sent me. [14:25] These things have I spoken unto you, being [yet] present with you.[14:26] But the Comforter, [which is] the Holy Ghost, whom the Father will send in my name, he shall teach you all things, and bring all things to your remembrance, whatsoever I have said unto you. [14:27] Peace I leave with you, my peace I give unto you: not as the world giveth, give I unto you. Let not your heart be troubled, neither let it be afraid. [14:28] Ye have heard how I said unto you, I go away, and come [again] unto you. If ye loved me, ye would rejoice, because I said, I go unto the Father: for my Father is greater than I. [14:29] And now I have told you before it come to pass, that, when it is come to pass, ye might believe. [14:30] Hereafter I will not talk much with you: for the prince of this world cometh, and hath nothing in me.[14:31] But that the world may know that I love the Father; and as the Father gave me commandment, even so I do. Arise, let us go hence.

Chapter 15

[15:1] I am the true vine, and my Father is the husbandman. [15:2] Every branch in me that beareth not fruit he taketh away: and every [branch] that beareth fruit, he purgeth it, that it may bring forth more fruit. [15:3] Now ye are clean through the word which I have spoken unto you. [15:4] Abide in me, and I in you. As the branch cannot bear fruit of itself, except it abide in the vine; no more can ye, except ye abide in me. [15:5] I am the vine, ye [are] the branches: He that abideth in me, and I in him, the same bringeth forth much fruit: for without me ye can do nothing.[15:6] If a man abide not in me, he is cast forth as a branch, and is withered; and men gather them, and cast [them] into the fire, and they are burned. [15:7] If ye abide in me, and my words abide in you, ye shall ask what ye will, and it shall be done unto you. [15:8] Herein is my Father glorified, that ye bear much fruit; so shall ye be my disciples. [15:9] As the Father hath loved me, so have I loved you: continue ye in my love. [15:10] If ye keep my commandments, ye shall abide in my love; even as I have kept my Father's commandments, and abide in his love.[15:11] These things have I spoken unto you, that my joy might remain in you, and [that] your joy might be full.[15:12] This is my commandment, That ye love one another, as I have loved you. [15:13] Greater love hath no man than this, that a man lay down his life for his friends.[15:14] Ye are my friends, if ye do whatsoever I command you. [15:15] Henceforth I call you not servants; for the servant knoweth not what his lord doeth: but I have called you friends; for all things that I have heard of my Father I have made known unto you. [15:16] Ye have not chosen me, but I have chosen you, and ordained you, that ye should go and bring forth fruit, and [that] your fruit should remain: that whatsoever ye shall ask of the Father in my name, he may give it you. [15:17] These things I command you, that ye love one another. [15:18] If the world hate you, ye know that [it hated] me before it hated you. [15:19] If ye were of the world, the world would love his own: but because ye are not of the world, but I have chosen you out of the world, therefore the world hateth you. [15:20] Remember the word that I said unto you, The servant is not greater than his lord. If they have persecuted me, they will also persecute you; if they have kept my saying, they will keep yours also.[15:21] But all these things will they do unto you for my .[15:22] If I had not come and spoken unto them, they had not had sin: but now they have no cloke for their sin.[15:23] He that hateth me hateth my Father also. [15:24] If I had not done among them the works which none other man did, they had not had sin: but now have they both seen and hated both me and my Father. [15:25] But [this cometh to pass,] that the word might be fulfilled that is written in their law, They hated me without a cause. [15:26] But when the Comforter is come, whom I will send unto you from the Father, [even] the Spirit of truth, which proceedeth from the

Father, he shall testify of me: [15:27] And ye also shall bear witness, because ye have been with me from the beginning.

Chapter 16

[16:1] These things have I spoken unto you, that ye should not be offended. [16:2] They shall put you out of the synagogues: yea, the time cometh, that whosoever killeth you will think that he doeth God service. [16:3] And these things will they do unto you, because they have not known the Father, nor me. [16:4] But these things have I told you, that when the time shall come, ye may remember that I told you of them. And these things I said not unto you at the beginning, because I was with you. [16:5] But now I go my way to him that sent me; and none of you asketh me, Whither goest thou? [16:6] But because I have said these things unto you, sorrow hath filled your heart. [16:7] Nevertheless I tell you the truth; It is expedient for you that I go away: for if I go not away, the Comforter will not come unto you; but if I depart, I will send him unto you. [16:8] And when he is come, he will reprove the world of sin, and of righteousness, and of judgment: [16:9] Of sin, because they believe not on me; [16:10] Of righteousness, because I go to my Father, and ye see me no more; [16:11] Of judgment, because the prince of this world is judged.[16:12] I have yet many things to say unto you, but ye cannot bear them now. [16:13] Howbeit when he, the Spirit of truth, is come, he will guide you into all truth: for he shall not speak of himself; but whatsoever he shall hear,[that] shall he speak: and he will shew you things to come.[16:14] He shall glorify me: for he shall receive of mine, and shall shew [it] unto you. [16:15] All things that the Father hath are mine: therefore said I, that he shall take of mine, and shall shew [it] unto you. [16:16] A little while, and ye shall not see me: and again, a little while, and ye shall see me, because I go to the Father. [16:17] Then said [some] of his disciples among themselves, What is this that he saith unto us, A little while, and ye shall not see me: and again, a little while, and ye shall see me: and, Because I go to the Father? [16:18] They said therefore, What is this that he saith, A little while? we cannot tell what he saith.[16:19] Now Jesus knew that they were desirous to ask him, and said unto them, Do ye enquire among yourselves of that I said, A little while, and ye shall not see me: and again, a little while, and ye shall see me? [16:20] Verily, verily, I say unto you, That ye shall weep and lament, but the world shall rejoice: and ye shall be sorrowful, but your sorrow shall be turned into joy. [16:21] A woman when she is in travail hath sorrow, because her hour is come: but as soon as she is delivered of the child, she remembereth no more the anguish, for joy that a man is born into the world.[16:22] And ye now therefore have sorrow: but I will see you again, and your heart shall rejoice, and your joy no man taketh from you. [16:23] And in that day ye shall ask me nothing. Verily, verily, I say unto you, Whatsoever ye shall ask the Father in my name, he will give [it] you. [16:24] Hitherto have ye asked nothing in my name: ask, and ye shall receive, that your joy may be full. [16:25] These things have I spoken unto you in proverbs: but the time cometh, when I shall no more speak unto you in proverbs, but I shall shew you plainly of the Father. [16:26] At that day ye shall ask in my name: and I say not unto you, that I will pray the Father for you: [16:27] For the Father himself loveth you, because ye have loved me, and have believed that I came out from God. [16:28] I came forth from the Father, and am come into the world: again, I leave the world, and go to the Father. [16:29] His disciples said unto him, Lo, now speakest thou plainly, and speakest no proverb. [16:30] Now are we sure that thou knowest all things, and needest not that any man should ask thee: by this we believe that thou camest forth from God. [16:31] Jesus answered them, Do ye now believe? [16:32] Behold, the hour cometh, yea, is now come, that ye shall be scattered, every man to his own, and shall leave me alone: and yet I am not alone, because the Father is with me. [16:33] These things I have spoken unto you, that in me ye might have peace. In the world ye shall have tribulation: but be of good cheer; I have overcome the world.

Chapter 17

[17:1] These words spake Jesus, and lifted up his eyes to heaven, and said, Father, the hour is come; glorify thy Son, that thy Son also may glorify thee: [17:2] As thou hast given him power over all flesh, that he should give eternal life to as many as thou hast given him. [17:3] And this is life eternal, that they might know thee the only true God, and Jesus Christ, whom thou hast sent. [17:4] I have glorified thee on the earth: I have finished the work which thou gavest me to do. [17:5] And now, O

Father, glorify thou me with thine own self with the glory which I had with thee before the world was. [17:6] I have manifested thy name unto the men which thou gavest me out of the world: thine they were, and thou gavest them me; and they have kept thy word. [17:7] Now they have known that all things whatsoever thou hast given me are of thee. [17:8] For I have given unto them the words which thou gavest me; and they have received [them,] and have known surely that I came out from thee, and they have believed that thou didst send me. [17:9] I pray for them: I pray not for the world, but for them which thou hast given me; for they are thine.[17:10] And all mine are thine, and thine are mine; and I am glorified in them. [17:11] And now I am no more in the world, but these are in the world, and I come to thee. Holy Father, keep through thine own name those whom thou hast given me, that they may be one, as we [are.][17:12] While I was with them in the world, I kept them in thy name: those that thou gavest me I have kept, and none of them is lost, but the son of perdition; that the scripture might be fulfilled.[17:13] And now come I to thee; and these things I speak in the world, that they might have my joy fulfilled in themselves. [17:14] I have given them thy word; and the world hath hated them, because they are not of the world, even as I am not of the world. [17:15] I pray not that thou shouldest take them out of the world, but that thou shouldest keep them from the evil. [17:16] They are not of the world, even as I am not of the world. [17:17] Sanctify them through thy truth: thy word is truth. [17:18] As thou hast sent me into the world, even so have I also sent them into the world. [17:19] And for their sakes I sanctify myself, that they also might be sanctified through the truth. [17:20] Neither pray I for these alone, but for them also which shall believe on me through their word; [17:21] That they all may be one; as thou, Father, [art] in me, and I in thee, that they also may be one in us: that the world may believe that thou hast sent me. [17:22] And the glory which thou gavest me I have given them; that they may be one, even as we are one: [17:23] I in them, and thou in me, that they may be made perfect in one; and that the world may know that thou hast sent me, and hast loved them, as thou hast loved me. [17:24] Father, I will that they also, whom thou hast given me, be with me where I am; that they may behold my glory, which thou hast given me: for thou lovedst me before the foundation of the world. [17:25] O righteous Father, the world hath not known thee: but I have known thee, and these have known that thou hast sent me. [17:26] And I have declared unto them thy name, and will declare [it:] that the love wherewith thou hast loved me may be in them, and I in them.

Chapter 18

[18:1] When Jesus had spoken these words, he went forth with his disciples over the brook Cedron, where was a garden, into the which he entered, and his disciples. [18:2] And Judas also, which betrayed him, knew the place: for Jesus ofttimes resorted thither with his disciples. [18:3] Judas then, having received a band [of men] and officers from the chief priests and

Pharisees, cometh thither with lanterns and torches and weapons. [18:4] Jesus therefore, knowing all things that should come upon him, went forth, and said unto them, Whom seek ye? [18:5] They answered him, Jesus of Nazareth. Jesus saith unto them, I am [he.] And Judas also, which betrayed him, stood with them.[18:6] As soon then as he had said unto them, I am [he,] they went backward, and fell to the ground. [18:7] Then asked he them again, Whom seek ye? And they said, Jesus of Nazareth. [18:8] Jesus answered, I have told you that I am [he:] if therefore ye seek me, let these go their way:[18:9] That the saying might be fulfilled, which he spake, Of them which thou gavest me have I lost none. [18:10] Then Simon Peter having a sword drew it, and smote the high priest's servant, and cut off his right ear. The servant's name was Malchus. [18:11] Then said Jesus unto Peter, Put up thy sword into the sheath: the cup which my Father hath given me, shall I not drink it? [18:12] Then the band and the captain and officers of the Jews took Jesus, and bound him, [18:13] And led him away to Annas first; for he was father in law to Caiaphas, which was the high priest that same year. [18:14] Now Caiaphas was he, which gave counsel to the Jews, that it was expedient that one man should die for the people.

[18:15] And Simon Peter followed Jesus, and [so did] another disciple: that disciple was known unto the high priest, and went in with Jesus into the palace of the high priest. [18:16] But Peter stood at the door without. Then went out that other disciple, which was known unto the high priest, and spake unto her that kept the door, and brought in Peter. [18:17] Then saith the damsel that kept the door unto Peter, Art not thou also [one] of this man's disciples? He saith, I am not. [18:18] And the servants and officers stood there, who had made a fire of coals; for it was cold: and they warmed themselves: and Peter stood with them, and warmed himself.

[18:19] The high priest then asked Jesus of his disciples, and of his doctrine. [18:20] Jesus answered him, I spake openly to the world; I ever taught in the synagogue, and in the temple, whither the Jews always resort; and in secret have I said nothing. [18:21] Why askest thou me? ask them which heard me, what I have said unto them: behold, they know what I said. [18:22] And when he had thus spoken, one of the officers which stood by struck Jesus with the palm of his hand, saying, Answerest thou the high priest so?[18:23] Jesus answered him, If I have spoken evil, bear witness of the evil: but if well, why smitest thou me?[18:24] Now Annas had sent him bound unto Caiaphas the high priest. [18:25] And Simon Peter stood and warmed himself. They said therefore unto him, Art not thou also [one] of his disciples? He denied [it,] and said, I am not. [18:26] One of the servants of the high priest, being [his] kinsman whose ear Peter cut off, saith, Did not I see thee in the garden with him? [18:27] Peter then denied again: and immediately the cock crew.

[18:28] Then led they Jesus from Caiaphas unto the hall of judgment: and it was early; and they themselves went not into the judgment hall, lest they should be defiled;

but that they might eat the passover. [18:29] Pilate then went out unto them, and said, What accusation bring ye against this man? [18:30] They answered and said unto him, If he were not a malefactor, we would not have delivered him up unto thee. [18:31] Then said Pilate unto them, Take ye him, and judge him according to your law. The Jews therefore said unto him, It is not lawful for us to put any man to death:[18:32] That the saying of Jesus might be fulfilled, which he spake, signifying what death he should die. [18:33] Then Pilate entered into the judgment hall again, and called Jesus, and said unto him, Art thou the King of the Jews?[18:34] Jesus answered him, Sayest thou this thing of thyself, or did others tell it thee of me? [18:35] Pilate answered, Am I a Jew? Thine own nation and the chief priests have delivered thee unto me: what hast thou done?[18:36] Jesus answered, My kingdom is not of this world: if my kingdom were of this world, then would my servants fight, that I should not be delivered to the Jews: but now is my kingdom not from hence. [18:37] Pilate therefore said unto him, Art thou a king then? Jesus answered, Thou sayest that I am a king. To this end was I born, and for this cause came I into the world, that I should bear witness unto the truth. Every one that is of the truth heareth my voice.[18:38] Pilate saith unto him, What is truth? And when he had said this, he went out again unto the Jews, and saith unto them, I find in him no fault [at all.][18:39] But ye have a custom, that I should release unto you one at the passover: will ye therefore that I release unto you the King of the Jews?

[18:40] Then cried they all again, saying, Not this man, but Barabbas. Now Barabbas was a robber.

Chapter 19

[19:1] Then Pilate therefore took Jesus, and scourged [him.][19:2] And the soldiers platted a crown of thorns, and put [it] on his head, and they put on him a purple robe,[19:3] And said, Hail, King of the Jews! and they smote him with their hands. [19:4] Pilate therefore went forth again, and saith unto them, Behold, I bring him forth to you, that ye may know that I find no fault in him. [19:5] Then came Jesus forth, wearing the crown of thorns, and the purple robe. And [Pilate] saith unto them, Behold the man![19:6] When the chief priests therefore and officers saw him, they cried out, saying, Crucify [him,] crucify [him.] Pilate saith unto them, Take ye him, and crucify [him:] for I find no fault in him. [19:7] The Jews answered him, We have a law, and by our law he ought to die, because he made himself the Son of God.

[19:8] When Pilate therefore heard that saying, he was the more afraid; [19:9] And went again into the judgment hall, and saith unto Jesus, Whence art thou? But Jesus gave him no answer. [19:10] Then saith Pilate unto him, Speakest thou not unto me? knowest thou not that I have power to crucify thee, and have power to release thee?[19:11] Jesus answered, Thou couldest have no power [at all] against me, except it were given thee from above: therefore he that delivered me unto thee hath the greater sin.[19:12] And from thenceforth

Pilate sought to release him: but the Jews cried out, saying, If thou let this man go, thou art not Caesar's friend: whosoever maketh himself a king speaketh against Caesar.

[19:13] When Pilate therefore heard that saying, he brought Jesus forth, and sat down in the judgment seat in a place that is called the Pavement, but in the Hebrew, Gabbatha. [19:14] And it was the preparation of the passover, and about the sixth hour: and he saith unto the Jews, Behold your King! [19:15] But they cried out, Away with [him,] away with [him,] crucify him. Pilate saith unto them, Shall I crucify your King? The chief priests answered, We have no king but Caesar. [19:16] Then delivered he him therefore unto them to be crucified. And they took Jesus, and led [him] away. [19:17] And he bearing his cross went forth into a place called [the place] of a skull, which is called in the Hebrew Golgotha: [19:18] Where they crucified him, and two others with him, on either side one, and Jesus in the midst.

[19:19] And Pilate wrote a title, and put [it] on the cross. And the writing was, JESUS OF NAZARETH THE KING OF THE JEWS. [19:20] This title then read many of the Jews: for the place where Jesus was crucified was nigh to the city: and it was written in Hebrew, [and] Greek, [and] Latin. [19:21] Then said the chief priests of the Jews to Pilate, Write not, The King of the Jews; but that he said, I am King of the Jews. [19:22] Pilate answered, What I have written I have written.

[19:23] Then the soldiers, when they had crucified Jesus, took his garments, and made four parts, to every soldier a part; and also [his] coat: now the coat was without seam, woven from the top throughout. [19:24] They said therefore among themselves, Let us not rend it, but cast lots for it, whose it shall be: that the scripture might be fulfilled, which saith, They parted my raiment among them, and for my vesture they did cast lots. These things therefore the soldiers did.

[19:25] Now there stood by the cross of Jesus his mother, and his mother's sister, Mary the [wife] of Cleophas, and Mary Magdalene. [19:26] When Jesus therefore saw his mother, and the disciple standing by, whom he loved, he saith unto his mother, Woman, behold thy son! [19:27] Then saith he to the disciple, Behold thy mother! And from that hour that disciple took her unto his own [home][19:28] After this, Jesus knowing that all things were now accomplished, that the scripture might be fulfilled, saith, I thirst. [19:29] Now there was set a vessel full of vinegar: and they filled a spunge with vinegar, and put [it] upon hyssop, and put [it] to his mouth. [19:30] When Jesus therefore had received the vinegar, he said, It is finished: and he bowed his head, and gave up the ghost. [19:31] The Jews therefore, because it was the preparation, that the bodies should not remain upon the cross on the sabbath day,(for that sabbath day was an high day,) besought Pilate that their legs might be broken, and [that] they might be taken away. [19:32] Then came the soldiers, and brake the legs of the first, and of the other which was crucified with him.[19:33] But when they came to Jesus, and saw that he was dead already, they brake not his legs: [19:34] But one of the soldiers with a spear pierced his side, and forthwith came there out blood and water. [19:35] And he that saw [it] bare record, and his record is true: and he knoweth that he saith true, that ye might believe. [19:36] For these things were done, that the scripture should be fulfilled, A bone of him shall not be broken. [19:37] And again another scripture saith, They shall look on him whom they pierced. Pilate that he might take away the body of Jesus: and Pilate gave [him] leave. He came therefore, and took the body of Jesus. [19:39] And there came also Nicodemus, which at the first came to Jesus by night, and brought a mixture of myrrh and aloes, about an hundred pound [weight.][19:40] Then took they the body of Jesus, and wound it in linen clothes with the spices, as the manner of the Jews is to bury.[19:41] Now in the place where he was crucified there was a garden; and in the garden a new sepulchre, wherein was never man yet laid. [19:42] There laid they Jesus therefore because of the Jews' preparation [day;] for the sepulchre was nigh at hand.

Chapter 20

[20:1] The first [day] of the week cometh Mary Magdalene early, when it was yet dark, unto the sepulchre, and seeth the stone taken away from the sepulchre. [20:2] Then she runneth, and cometh to Simon Peter, and to the other disciple, whom Jesus loved, and saith unto them, They have taken away the Lord out of the sepulchre, and we know not where they have laid him. [20:3] Peter therefore went forth, and that other disciple, and came to the sepulchre. [20:4] So they ran both together: and the other disciple did outrun Peter, and came first to the sepulchre.[20:5] And he stooping down, [and looking in,] saw the linen clothes lying; yet went he not in. [20:6] Then cometh Simon Peter following him, and went into the sepulchre, and seeth the linen clothes lie, [20:7] And the napkin, that was about his head, not lying with the linen clothes, but wrapped together in a place by itself. [20:8] Then went in also that other disciple, which came first to the sepulchre, and he saw, and believed. [20:9] For as yet they knew not the scripture, that he must rise again from the dead. [20:10] Then the disciples went away again unto their own home.

[20:11] But Mary stood without at the sepulchre weeping: and as she wept, she stooped down, [and looked] into the sepulchre, [20:12] And seeth two angels in white sitting, the one at the head, and the other at the feet, where the body of Jesus had lain. [20:13] And they say unto her, Woman, why weepest thou? She saith unto them, Because they have taken away my Lord, and I know not where they have laid him. [20:14] And when she had thus said, she turned herself back, and saw Jesus standing, and knew not that it was Jesus. [20:15] Jesus saith unto her, Woman, why weepest thou? whom seekest thou? She, supposing him to be the gardener, saith unto him, Sir, if thou have borne him hence, tell me where thou hast laid him, and I will take him away. [20:16] Jesus saith unto her, Mary. She turned herself, and saith unto him, Rabboni; which is to say, Master. [20:17] Jesus saith unto her, Touch me not; for I am not yet ascended to my Father: but go to my brethren, and say unto them, I ascend unto my Father, and your Father; and [to] my God, and your God. [20:18] Mary Magdalene came and told the disciples that she had seen the Lord, and [that] he had spoken these things unto her.

[20:19] Then the same day at evening, being the first [day] of the week, when the doors were shut where the disciples were assembled for fear of the Jews, came Jesus and stood in the midst, and saith unto them, Peace [be] unto you. [20:20] And when he had so said, he shewed unto them [his] hands and his side. Then were the disciples glad, when they saw the Lord. [20:21] Then said Jesus to them again, Peace [be] unto you: as [my] Father hath sent me, even so send I you. [20:22] And when he had said this, he breathed on [them,] and saith unto them, Receive ye the Holy Ghost: [20:23] Whose soever sins ye remit, they are remitted unto them; [and] whose soever [sins] ye retain, they are retained.

[20:24] But Thomas, one of the twelve, called Didymus, was not with them when Jesus came. [20:25] The other disciples therefore said unto him, We have seen the Lord. But he said unto them, Except I shall see in his hands the print of the nails, and put my finger into the print of the nails, and thrust my hand into his side, I will not believe.

[20:26] And after eight days again his disciples were within, and Thomas with them: [then] came Jesus, the doors being shut, and stood in the midst, and said, Peace [be] unto you. [20:27] Then saith he to Thomas, reach hither thy finger, and behold my hands; and reach hither thy hand, and thrust [it] into my side: and be not faithless, but believing.[20:28] And Thomas answered and said unto him, My Lord and my God. [20:29] Jesus saith unto him, Thomas, because thou hast seen me, thou hast believed: blessed [are] they that have not seen, and [yet] have believed.

[20:30] And many other signs truly did Jesus in the presence of his disciples, which are not written in this book:[20:31] But these are written, that ye might believe that Jesus is the Christ, the Son of God; and that believing ye might have life through his name.

[21:1] After these things Jesus shewed himself again to the disciples at the sea of Tiberias; and on this wise shewed he [himself.][21:2] There were together Simon Peter, and Thomas called Didymus, and Nathanael of Cana in Galilee, and the [sons] of Zebedee, and two other of his disciples.[21:3] Simon Peter saith unto them, I go a fishing. They say unto him, We also go with thee. They went forth, and entered into a ship immediately; and that night they caught nothing. [21:4] But when the morning was now come, Jesus stood on the shore: but the disciples knew not that it was Jesus. [21:5] Then Jesus saith unto them, Children, have ye any meat? They answered him, No. [21:6] And he said unto them, Cast the net on the right side of the ship, and ye shall find. They cast therefore, and now they were not able to draw it for the multitude of fishes. [21:7] Therefore that disciple whom Jesus loved saith unto Peter, It is the Lord. Now when Simon Peter heard that it was the Lord, he girt [his] fisher's coat [unto him,] (for he was naked,) and did cast himself into the sea. [21:8] And the other disciples came in a little ship; (for they were not far from land, but as it were two hundred cubits,) dragging the net with fishes. [21:9] As soon then as they were come to land, they saw a fire of coals there, and fish laid thereon, and bread. [21:10] Jesus saith unto them, Bring of the fish which ye have now caught. [21:11] Simon Peter went up, and drew the net to land full of great fishes, and hundred and fifty and three: and for all there were so many, yet was not the net broken. [21:12] Jesus saith unto them, Come [and] dine. And none of the disciples durst ask him, Who art thou? knowing that it was the Lord. [21:13] Jesus then cometh, and taketh bread, and giveth them, and fish likewise. [21:14] This is now the third time that Jesus shewed himself to his disciples, after that he was risen from the dead.

[21:15] So when they had dined, Jesus saith to Simon Peter, Simon, [son] of Jonas, lovest thou me more than these? He saith unto him, Yea, Lord; thou knowest that I love thee. He saith unto him, Feed my lambs. [21:16] He saith to him again the second time, Simon, [son] of Jonas, lovest thou me? He saith unto him, Yea, Lord; thou knowest that I love thee. He saith unto him, Feed my sheep. [21:17] He saith unto him the third time,

Simon, [son] of Jonas, lovest thou me? Peter was grieved because he said unto him the third time, Lovest thou me? And he said unto him, Lord, thou knowest all things; thou knowest that I love thee. Jesus saith unto him, Feed my sheep. [21:18] Verily, verily, I say unto thee, When thou wast young, thou girdedst thyself, and walkedst whither thou wouldest: but when thou shalt be old, thou shalt stretch forth thy hands, and another shall gird thee, and carry [thee] whither thou wouldest not. [21:19] This spake he, signifying by what death he should glorify God. And when he had spoken this, he saith unto him, Follow me. [21:20] Then Peter, turning about, seeth the disciple whom Jesus loved following; which also leaned on his breast at supper, and said, Lord, which is he that betrayeth thee? [21:21] Peter seeing him saith to Jesus, Lord, and what [shall] this man [do?][21:22] Jesus saith unto him, If I will that he tarry till I come, what [is that] to thee? follow thou me. [21:23] Then went this saying abroad among the brethren, that that disciple should not die: yet Jesus said not unto him, He shall not die; but, If I will that he tarry till I come, what [is that] to thee? [21:24] This is the disciple which testifieth of these things, and wrote these things: and we know that his testimony is true.[21:25] And there are also many other things which Jesus did, the which, if they should be written every one, I suppose that even the world itself could not contain the books that should be written. Amen.

AUTHOR'S BRIEF BIO & CONTACT

Charles Mwewa (LLB. BA. Education. BA. Legal Studies. Cert. Law. DIBM. LLM Cand.) is a Dad, author, lawyer, educator, and moral and social influencer. Mwewa is the author of 30 books and counting in all genres – fiction (novels), non-fiction and poetry. Mwewa, his wife, and their three girls, reside in the Capital City of Ottawa, Canada.

Email address:
lawdebar@gmail.com

Facebook:
www.facebook.com/charlesmwewa

Twitter:
https://twitter.com/BooksMwewa

Instagram:
instagram.com/mwewabooks/?hl=en

Author's website:
https://www.charlesmwewa.com

To order this book online:
https://www.amazon.com/dp/1988251893

INDEX

L

M

N

O

P

R

S

Made in the USA
Monee, IL
08 November 2026

68085075R00080